M A R Y   M C C L E A R Y   **A F T**

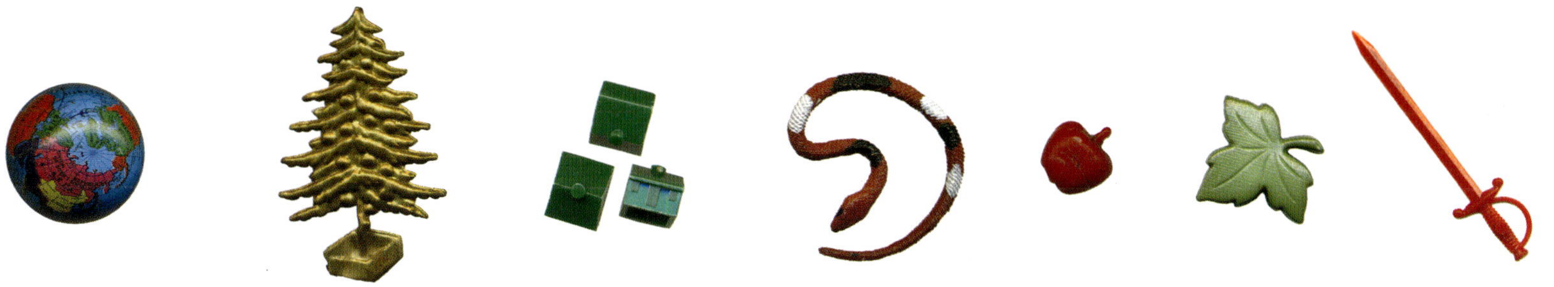

In Christian art, the square halo identified a living person presumed to be a saint. Square Halo Books is devoted to publishing works that present contextually sensitive biblical studies, and practical instruction consistent with the Doctrines of the Reformation. The goal of Square Halo Books is to provide materials useful for encouraging and equipping the saints.

Square Halo Books

P.O. Box 18954
Baltimore, MD 21206
www.SquareHaloBooks.com

ISBN 0-9785097-0-6

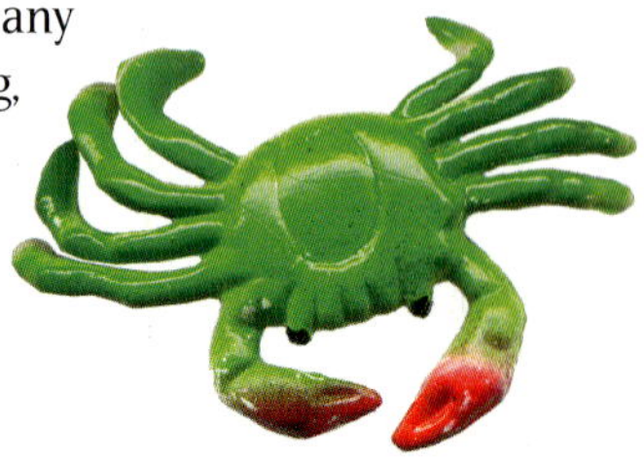

Printed in Korea

SOME THINGS ABOUT **MARY**

One of the great joys of staying in a career in the arts for a long time is the privilege of following the progress of an artist throughout their career. It has been my pleasure to follow Mary McCleary's career since shortly after her graduation from the Master's program at the University of Oklahoma and her employment at Stephen F. Austin State University in Nacogdoches.

Over those thirty years I have watched her work move from brightly colored prints with punny titles like *Hold Your Tongue,* through large-scale abstractions in paper, canvas and metal—a brief sojourn with clay—tentative beginnings in the art of construction which burgeoned into ever more sophisticated and complicated multi-media compositions—ultimately tackling the figure (nearly full scale) and complex narrative ideas—and most recently, full circle back to print-making, this time with no color and very serious content. It has been a joyous, albeit often challenging, ride also involving my serving as a model for two of her works.

It always pleases me to watch growth. In the case of many artists it is artistic, technically skillful growth. In the case of great artists it is also emotionally and intellectually challenging growth which propels the work forward and raises it to new heights. Mary has achieved that level of artistic, technical, emotional and intellectual sophistication all while raising a family and being an exceptional teacher—and doing so while living and working in small-town East Texas. Oh, and did I mention that along the way she has become a serious student of the Bible and of philosophical thought all the while listening to show tunes, cabaret and big-band music of the forties and fifties and watching film noir?

Over the three decades I have known her art, the progress from the word play of a 1970's silkscreen of a cat in the desert titled *Cat in Heat* to the foreboding image of a young girl falling through space in *Fallen Fallen Light Renew* (based on a William Blake poem) is a quantum leap of artistic faith as well as a personal growth in faith of equal proportions. Just as obviously, the ominous tenor of those poor souls in the boat drifting off into the darkness in *Between Darkness and Light* couldn't be further removed from the frothy sweetness of the1975 lithograph, *Texas Torte* with its floating confection in the shape of Texas. The silly subjects of youth have morphed into the fears and trepidations of mid-life and Technicolor has faded into black and white.

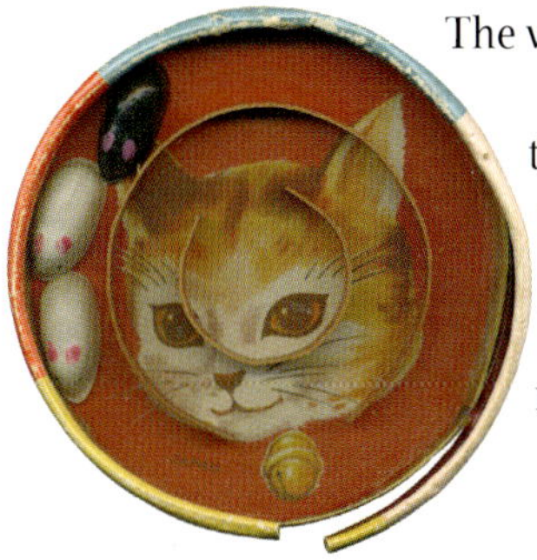

In much the same way, collages like *The Hoo-Haa* (2003) play off of adult fears. It serves as a literal interpretation of T.S. Eliot's words from *Sweeny Agnosties: Fragment of an Agon:*

When you're alone in the middle of the night and you wake
in a sweat and a hell of a fright
When you're alone in the middle of the bed and you wake
like someone hit you on the head
You've a cream of a nightmare and you've got the
hoo-ha's coming to you.

In an even more complex sense the work echoes the thought in another Eliot quote, "To those who have experienced the full horror of life, tragedy is still inadequate. In the end horror and laughter may be one."

Jerusalem, Athens, Alexandria, Vienna, London (2003) concerns itself with issues also confronted in the earlier *Children of the Apple Tree*—those of the myth of the Noble Savage and of an ongoing attraction to the primitive while we, ourselves, may not be so far removed from the primitive and from the fall of the Old Testament. The veneer of Civilization may be thinner than we think.

In a similar way, Mary's two most recent works revisit themes of the past and re-work them into concerns of the present. In *Sehnsucht* (German for nostalgia) we are reminded of the vanitas works Mary produced in the mid-1980's. In this case, however, the flower arrangement has gone over the top. It is beyond rococo and

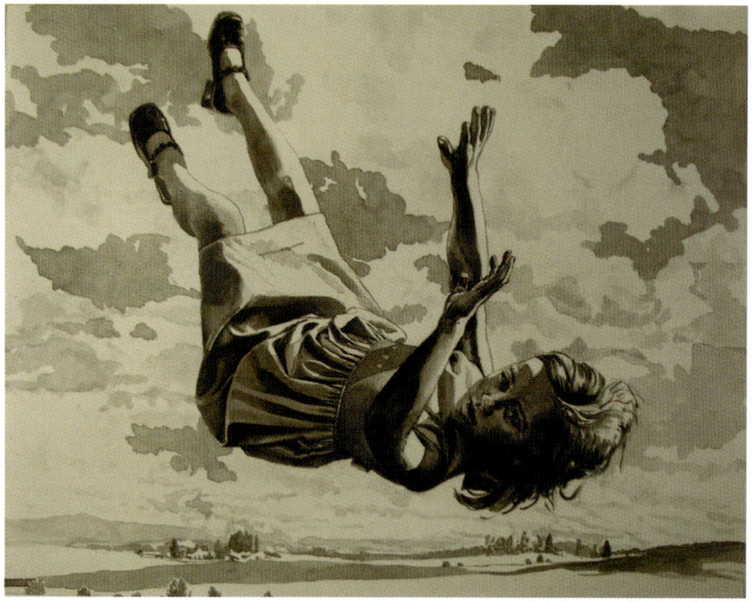

FALLEN, FALLEN, LIGHT RENEW 2005, 15 1/2 x 19 1/2
POLYMER GRAVURE CHINE COLLÉ

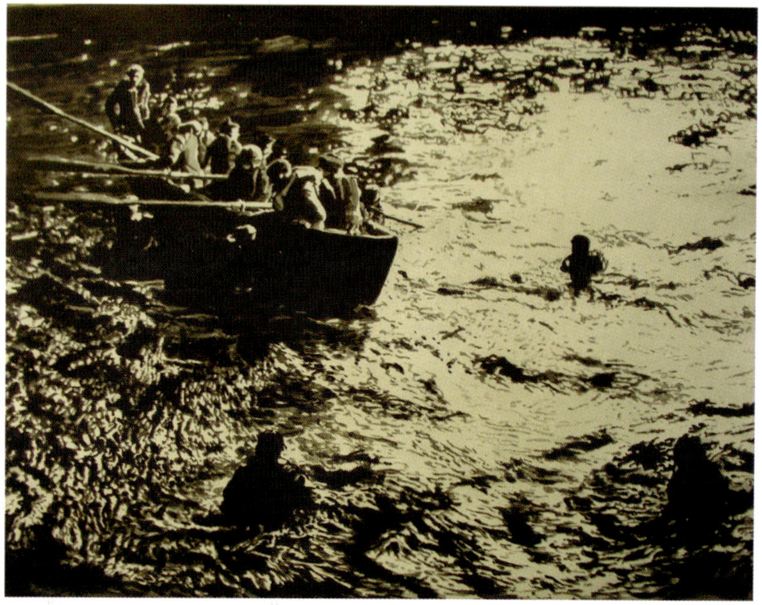

BETWEEN DARKNESS AND LIGHT 2005, 15 1/2 x 19 1/2
POLYMER GRAVURE CHINE COLLÉ

baroque, positively bursting off the surface in an explosion of color and texture absolutely dwarfing the interplay between the cat and bird and overshadowing the punnish irony of the postcard from "Paradise."

The Strange Dust of Our Actions Drifts and Settles Upon Us brings us back to the figure in nature, but, as with most of Mary's work, with a twist. The B-movie cowboy of our memories has been replaced with a Mary parody of a big haired Texas blond middle-aged cowgirl with a flashy diamond ring looking more like 40's ads of glamorous cowgirls selling all kinds of products. The underlying "dark side" of the image is the implication that for every action there is a consequence—that the effects of our actions fall around us like dust. Those flapping butterfly wings in the forest turning into raging winds, etc. Yet, hidden in the dust is a small Christmas toy—a kitschy clue to Mary's belief that there is a Christian solution to the problems she poses.

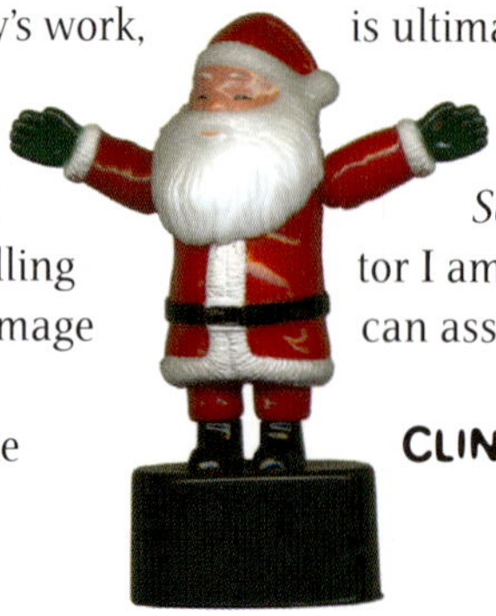

And therein may lie the key to much of Mary's work—that she is ultimately concerned with the ongoing theme in literature of our fall from grace and our flight from God and of His constant pursuit of us. As the model for the *The Good Samaritan* (1995), I am hopeful that she is right. As a curator I am confidant that He has guided Mary into making art that can assist him in his mission in a most amazing and unique way.

CLINT WILLOUR is the curator of the Galveston Arts Center.

MARY McCLEARY'S INGENIOUS SPOON

The first time I saw the art of Mary McCleary I went away talking about the stunning and affecting paintings I had seen. I had to keep correcting myself, knowing the works to be collages. By calling her works paintings I was testifying to their delightful surprise, the painterly impression she achieves through a pointillist fanaticism with mixed media. She is the Seurat of collage.

Then I found myself asking the question, why anyone would "paint" with glass beads, colored string, animal fur, kewpie doll eyes, costume jewels, foil, glitter, painted toothpicks, and the host of common, neglected, seemingly haphazard, and slyly chosen materials McCleary incorporates into her works.

Certainly, the art couldn't achieve such coruscating and endlessly-elaborated surfaces otherwise. But there's a basic awkwardness to such an approach; it's like setting out to dig a tunnel with a spoon. No one goes at it that way who isn't in prison. What escape might McCleary be so desperate to make? In the service of what freedom is she willing to devote such painstaking labor?

Then I noticed that often McCleary's recent works tell stories. She can employ a traditional iconographic vocabulary for narrative purposes. She wants us to reflect on the action represented, with close attention to its rendering as our means of discovering the artist's intention. She sees her work as a means of communicating, and she's not shy about giving us interpretive nudges with titles and accompanying text. The stories she tells are inspired by historical, literary, and biblical sources.

As someone who began studying art in the latter days of abstract expressionism, I was schooled to believe that paintings or even painterly collages should never tell a story. A canvas must be a self-existent world with no appeal to external references. So went the prevailing wisdom. In these postmodernist times the human figure has come back and along with it a degree of reference. Very rudimentary narratives have expanded on this, mostly taking up the artist's own identity, his relationship with the audience or the traditions of art itself and their economic basis. But narrative art that is informed by mythic structures—or meta-narratives, as they are now called—has yet to win wide acceptance. Narrative art implies that the artist and her audience share a common world—an idea that almost everyone in the arts doubts, if not ridicules.

Thus, Mary McCleary's ingenious spoon and her tunneling toward the light.

One of Mary McCleary's early works, from her student years, is called *Tongue-Tied* (1972). It's a watercolor of a mouth with the tongue hanging out knotted with a string. Many of the earliest images McCleary produced were similarly inspired by literalizing word-play. In one way *Tongue-tied* is only a piece of whimsy and evidence of a young artist's desire to find a means of jump-starting her imagination. McCleary often roamed the stacks of libraries (and still does), pulling volumes off the shelves whose literary value or images contained useful resonances. Yet, *Tongue-Tied* also serves as an emblem of impulses that were far deeper than the young artist knew and foreshadows her rebellion against many of the philosophic currents of contemporary art. For modernism and post-modernism can be seen as a denial of the creative word—the *Logos*—that brings all things into being. Because the arbiters of culture came to see the world as the product of chance, the human imagination's power to grasp the world in its essential being looked suspect. The imagination became a world unto itself—or a derivative of culture—and the artist's work a sign only of his own thoughts and dreams, without reference to a shared world. The honesty of the abstract expressionists demanded that any claims to the contrary be eschewed.

Mary McCleary always liked well-made objects whose craftsmanship resonated with her childhood exposure to good design. She grew up in Houston, her forebears Texans before statehood. Her father was an oil company executive. Her mother, grandmother and several aunts collected antiques. Early on they introduced Mary to the fascinating design in Chinese and Japanese porcelain, oriental rugs, and eighteenth century furniture and needlework. The virtues of various antiques were discussed at family gatherings, and after visiting

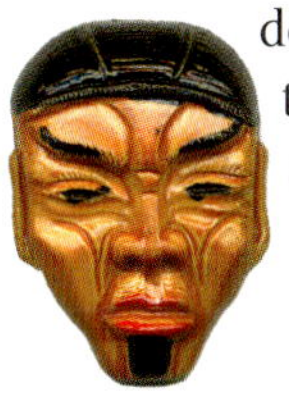

restored homes and museums, her sister Jan and she played docent. Her family's connoisseurship translated into Mary's childhood desire to become an artist. Mary's sense of how the well-made domestic object could become transcendent would assert itself in her mature work.

Mary prepared to be a working artist as an undergraduate at Texas Christian University and in graduate school at the University of Oklahoma, where she received an M.F.A. in drawing and print-making. Her art education occurred during the late 1960s and early 1970s when traditional disciplines such as drawing the figure, color theory, and composition fell into desuetude. One teacher in a drawing class told her that art had progressed to such a point that no one would ever draw the figure again. Time spent on such matters was wasted.

Mary McCleary was a modern, young woman—as an undergraduate she helped found NOW in Ft. Worth—but she was skeptical that great art could be made without skills. The great twentieth century fiction writer Flannery O'Connor said, "I have what passes for an education these days, but I am not fooled." McCleary felt something of the same. For this reason she concentrated much of her efforts on art history and print-making. The processes of intaglio and lithography required mastery. They rewarded skill and punished incompetence. If there were no standards any longer in the academy, the print-making processes themselves provided Mary a means of assessing her progress.

In 1975 McCleary joined the faculty at Stephen F. Austin State University. After exploring representational art while in school, her work as a young professional took a quantum leap forward, with a prodigious and profligate output of non-representational images. For the first time she let her childhood exposure to the decorative arts inform her work as much as favorite contemporary artists. Her work from this period was influenced by the forms of architectural drawing, the wall paintings of Pompeii and Herculeum, eighteenth and nineteenth century needlework and the painted surfaces of furniture. The less successful works employed a minimalist approach to space, but as the works became more dense and intricate in their design, the work improved dramatically. 1979's *Aubasson* and *Pomada,* saw McCleary elaborating the works' surfaces, giving these mixed-media pieces a degree of three-dimensionality. She accomplished this through scalloped paper folds, geometric designs of colorful sticks against painted backgrounds, and other playful strategies. The artist's mature identity was coming to shape under her hands. Her work was not yet the "Mary McCleary" we know at a glance, but she was on to something.

She was motivated to make the viewer linger and engage the work. The late 1970s and early 1980s were a time of booming art sales, with corporations snapping up the million-and-one decorative works to which abstract expressionism led. Every skyscraper foyer posted a would-be de Kooning; every hotel room a more polite Helen Frankenthaler. For the most part people registered these and passed on. Mary's mixed-media constructions offered a way to combine arresting images with a kinesthetic charge. She wanted to stop the audience in its tracks and feel the tactile pull of her surfaces. Like the cook in Isak Dinesen's short story, *Babette's Feast,* in which an exiled Parisian spends a fortune on preparing one meal for her otherwise indifferent village, McCleary wanted to serve up a visual feast.

Several contending ideas are to be seen in her early 1980's collages. A series of *Eden* paintings followed (1981–82), in which McCleary tried out the Romantic notion that the imagination provides a means of access to paradise. The artist's work aspires to be a moment of perfection.

The *Eden* paintings ran up against the realization in *I Am Dr. Frankenstein* (1984) that the imagination produces as many monsters as gardens. Instead of rejoicing in creating the artist may simply use it to exalt her ego.

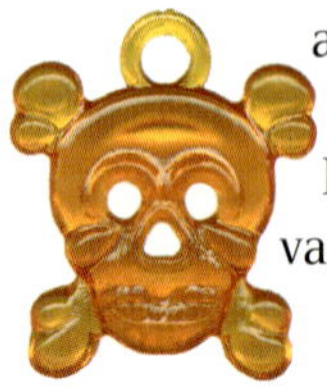

McCleary turned to a type of traditional still life painting that acknowledged the antinomies of *Eden* and *Frankenstein:* "Vanitas" paintings. These are based on the passage from Ecclesiastes: "Vanity of vanities, saith the Preacher, vanity of vanities; all is vanity" (1:2, KJV). Dutch painters of the northern

Renaissance, inspired by this passage, depicted skulls, rotting fruit, and broken glasses to remind householders that the world's glories pass. And yet, these paintings are among the most sumptuously beautiful pieces of art ever imagined. The contrast appealed powerfully to McCleary.

In the late 1970's and early 1980's, Mary McCleary began asking in a deeper way the perennial questions of meaning and purpose. She was happily married to architect Jerry Sutton, her professional career flourishing, and looking forward to having a family. But what was she doing devoting her life to making art? It would all come to dust.

Through much study McCleary's search led her to affirm the creative word—the *Logos*—who brought all things into being. She reaffirmed the faith of her Christian forebears. Her life and work might have only a contingent meaning that would soon pass, but she had been given the opportunity and privilege of entering into the creative process by which all things came to be.

Most contemporary artists who make such affirmations in their journeys arrive at this point in a sweat. Mary McCleary hardly hesitated. She did a piece for the Texas Sesquicentennial celebration in 1985, *Galveston Storm,* in which Christ's impaled feet walk over the waters and his hand reaches into the flood. Then another, *Alamo With St. Sebastian* (1985), that further expressed her understanding of suffering as redemptive. Her elaborated surfaces were now united with iconographic imagery and the implications of narrative. Mary McCleary, the artist we know today, was born. Her palette, which had previously wobbled from chalk tones to primary colors, now most often took its cues from the enameled fire of mosaic. The bold rusts, ebony, amethyst, chrysolite, and beryl blue and green of Ravenna's mosaics shine once again in McCleary's works. She had found her way to the hybrid collage-mosaic form that has characterized her mature work.

The reader may wonder whether I am still talking about works that are made out of rag board, glitter, sticks, painted toothpicks and toys that might be dispensed from gum ball machines. By alluding to the glories of Christian art in the past I seem to be gainsaying what appears to be the works' most insistent trait: their deliberate use of the most incidental materials imaginable. The radical contrast of the works' thematic ambitions and their humble materials points to the paradox at the heart of McCleary's vision. The world and we ourselves are composed of mere stuff, as contingent as any postmodernist might imagine, and yet when humankind reflects on life through the arts and when we ourselves review our own histories certain images snap into focus that speak the truth. The job of anyone who wants to communicate is to translate into mere stuff—whether images or written characters or sounds or pure sensation—meanings that we understand through the translator's arrangement or design. That's what makes all languages—oral, written, visual, and kinesthetic—*work.* McCleary's method forces the viewer to take into account the mystery of the incidental becoming significant and even transcendent. It's thoroughly contemporary and traditional simultaneously. Anyone who believes as McCleary does that the creative word was translated into mere flesh in Jesus sees the arts as having an incarnate character. What McCleary came to believe with all her heart, mind, soul, and strength translated itself into the work of her hands.

The collages in *After Paradise* are McCleary's most challenging to date. They convict and console like an Old Testament prophet shunted up in a tree stump but strangling out a message nevertheless.

As McCleary's work depends formally upon a radical disparity between the materials used and the intricacy of design, McCleary's work often relies thematically upon the shadow that falls between appearance and meaning. In *Nazi Pets* and *When Sparrows Fell* McCleary presents anti-parables of what happens when ideology embraces a violent disjuncture between the word and the world.

The Nazis hated the Jews not merely for trumped-up sociological reasons—control of the banking industry, etc.—but for their more potent threat: a word based religion that established fixed standards and militated against the Nazi's worldview of pure

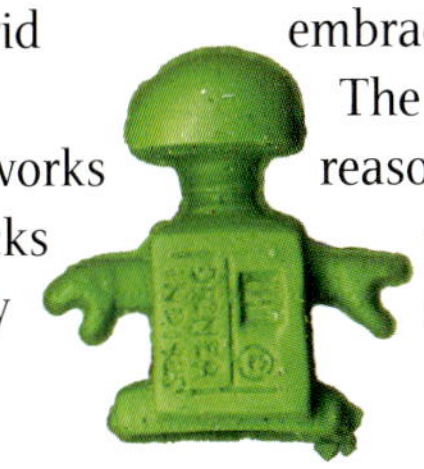

process. So the Nazis utterly ignored the inviolate dignity that belongs to the human person and worshiped the historical process that had brought them to power.

In much the same way Mao Zedong thought he could trump moral and natural law with mere human ingenuity and succeeded, as he did with everything he dreamed up, in producing slaughter.

Both pieces have visually exciting surfaces. *Nazi Pets* is exuberant and sly, while *When Sparrows Fell* has a festive violence. Both are ultimately as dark as the horror they depict.

McCleary's sense of tragedy is the more unsettling for its entrance through the back door of idealism. Think of Picasso's *Guernica.* We all want to raise our arms and scream when the bombs fall, but how should we react when a man's sentimentality about animals utterly vanquishes his humanity and effectively pledges him to evil?

Allegory of the Senses presents a sumptuous domestic scene, in which delights are on offer to sight, hearing, smell, touch, and taste. *Allegory* makes perhaps the best use to date of McCleary's love of Baroque art and its visual drama, with the *contrapposto* pose of the three characters playing a sensual and thematic role. Despite the rich furnishings and the work's gorgeous coloring in violet and mauve and Chinese yellow, the scene has a curiously muted affect. All three characters, the father and mother and their teenage son, are distracted. The father momentarily looks away from his book, the son plainly would prefer to take his phone call in private, and the mother, while searching after her son's gaze with her own, contents herself with petting the dog. They are turned toward one another and away simultaneously. Looking closely we see that moths flit about the scene, reminding us of the ultimate fate of silk and chintz. *Allegory* is the fulfillment of McCleary's long interest in Vanitas works. It shows a rich world bedeviled by impending decay and emotional distance.

In *Allegory* it is not incidental that the work is a collective portrait of the artist's family. The world is a broken place, the work tells us, and I, the artist, am part and parcel of that brokenness. One of the loveliest things about Mary McCleary's vision is that she rarely indulges in the luxury of setting herself apart from whatever experience she's depicting. There are touches of humanity with which the artist clearly identifies and calls the viewer to do the same even in the most horrific scenes. Judgment in her pictures is a judgment in which she is implicated.

The consoling paintings work with disparities that may be even more shocking than those present in the works with convicting themes. In *Lullaby* we wonder why the artist would show a bird about to plunge a worm into the gullet of a clubwoman. For any grown-up this is plainly offensive. And yet, the nicely-kempt lady opens her mouth and waits to receive the morsel as willingly as any baby bird. The circular plastic maze-toys scattered through the work's surface enclose scenes that speak of one type of oasis or another—provision in the midst of an otherwise desolate and dystopian world. The artist wants to remind us, it seems, of our radical dependency on the world's gifts; of Jesus' admonition: "Look at the birds of the air; they do not sow or reap or store away in barns, and yet your heavenly Father feeds them. Are you not much more valuable than they?" (Matt. 6:26).

After Paradise we are barred from storming the Gates of Eden through utopian fantasies and every merely human imagining, including the artist's own. We've fallen a long way since Eden, and, to judge by McCleary's *9.81 Meters Per Second Per Second,* our free-fall continues to accelerate. Her art evokes the horror we are so adapt at concocting and longs for the blessedness of a new earth characterized by love, justice, and peace—by God's redemption. Her work is an instance of how that process has already begun.

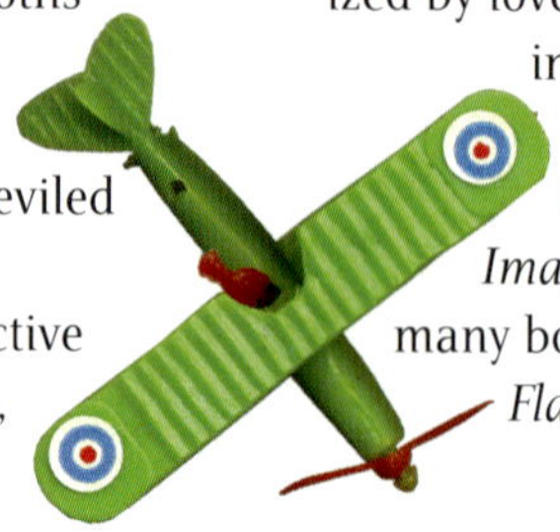

HAROLD FICKETT is the co-founder of the journal *Image*, a contributing editor of *GodSpy*, and the author of many books, including *The Living Christ, The Holy Fool,* and *Flannery O'Connor: Images of Grace.*

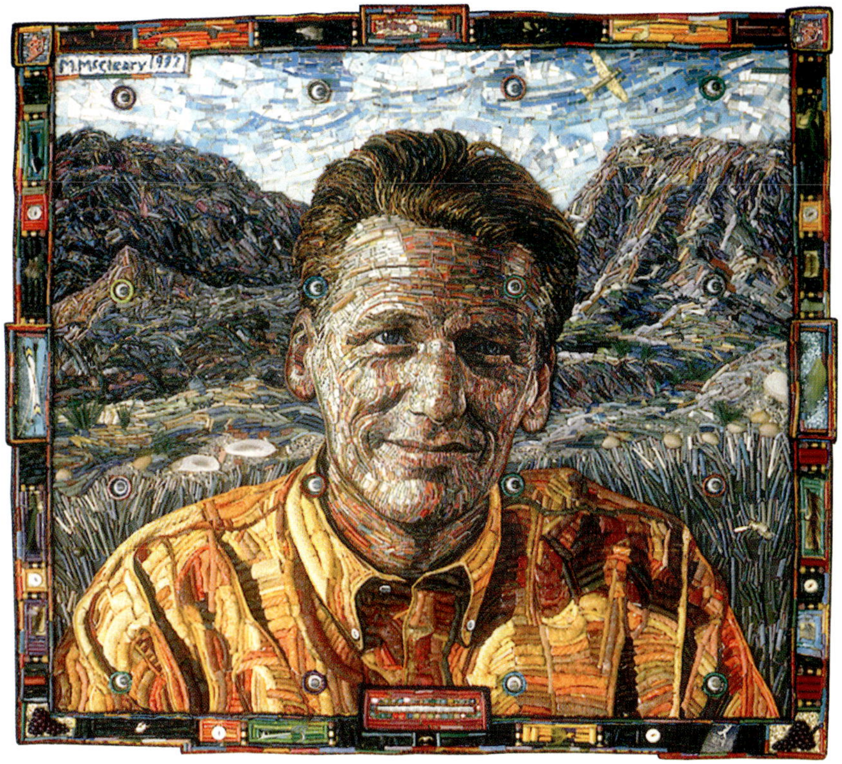

PORTRAIT OF JOHN MARMADUKE 1998, 27 x 30
MIXED MEDIA COLLAGE ON PAPER

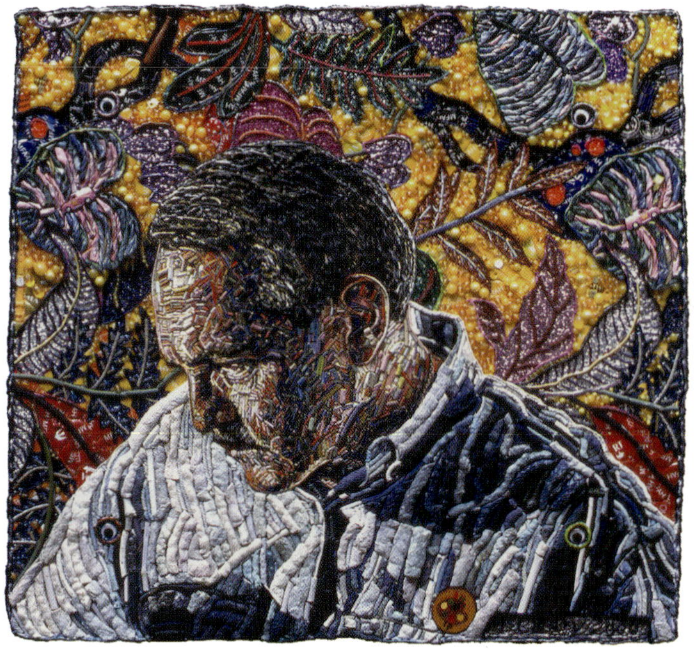

PORTRAIT OF CLINT WILLOUR 2000, 23 x 24 3/8
MIXED MEDIA COLLAGE ON PAPER

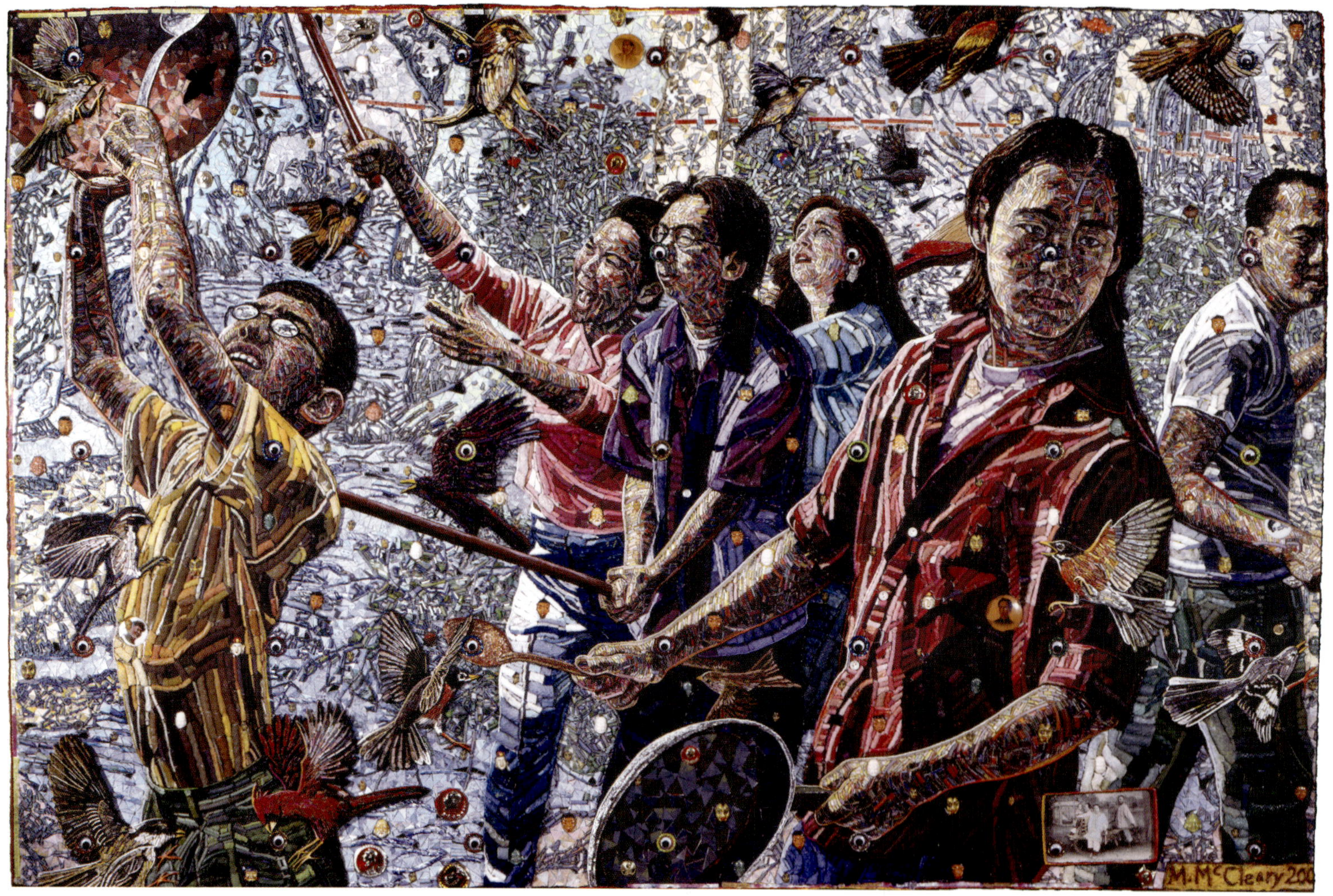

WHEN SPARROWS FELL 2001, 45 x 67 3/4
MIXED MEDIA COLLAGE ON PAPER

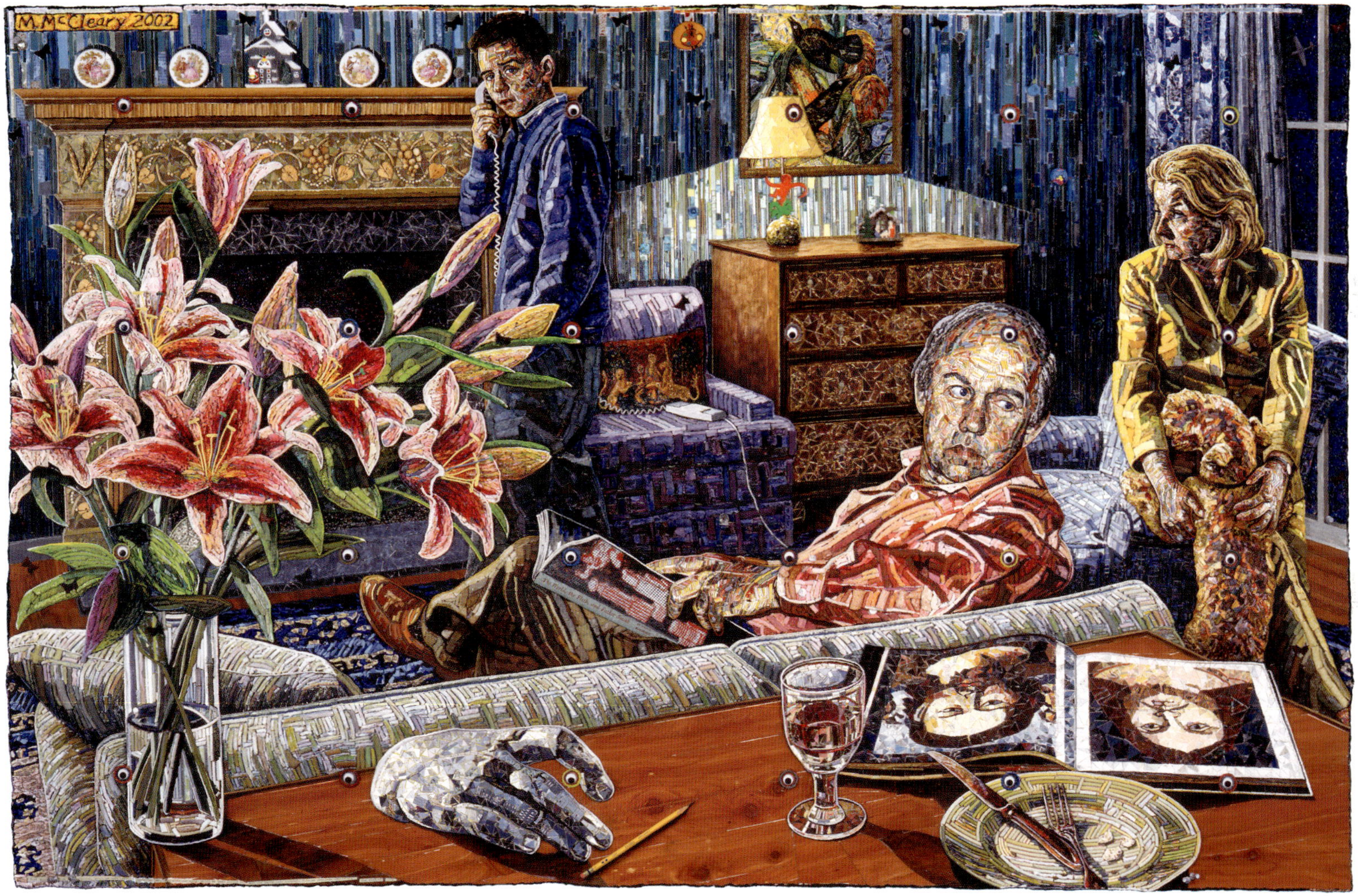

ALLEGORY OF THE SENSES 2002, 48 x 72 7/8
MIXED MEDIA COLLAGE ON PAPER

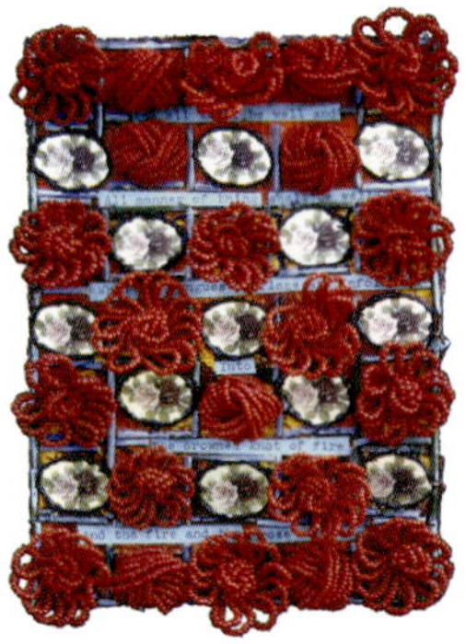

THE FIRE AND THE ROSE 2003, 7 3/8 x 5 1/2
MIXED MEDIA COLLAGE ON PAPER

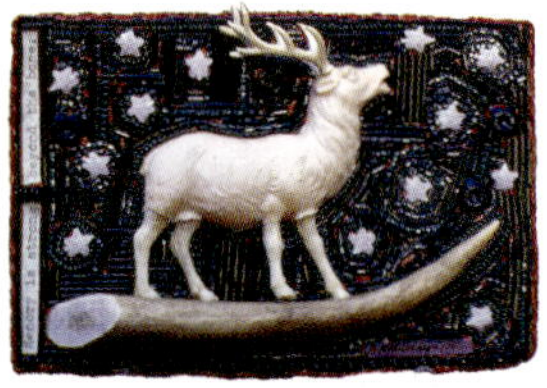

BEYOND THE BONE 2003, 4 1/4 x 6
MIXED MEDIA COLLAGE ON PAPER

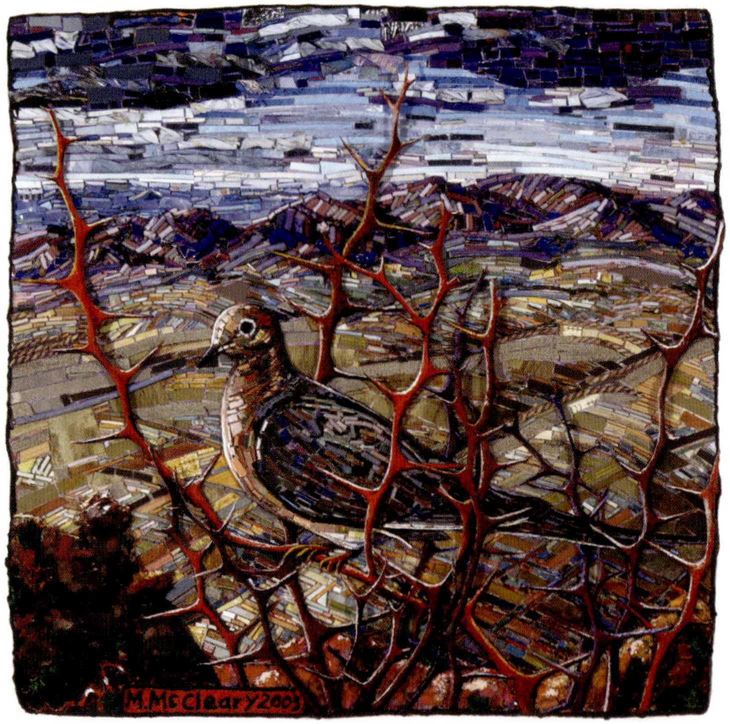

MOURNING DOVE 2003, 16 x 16
MIXED MEDIA COLLAGE ON PAPER

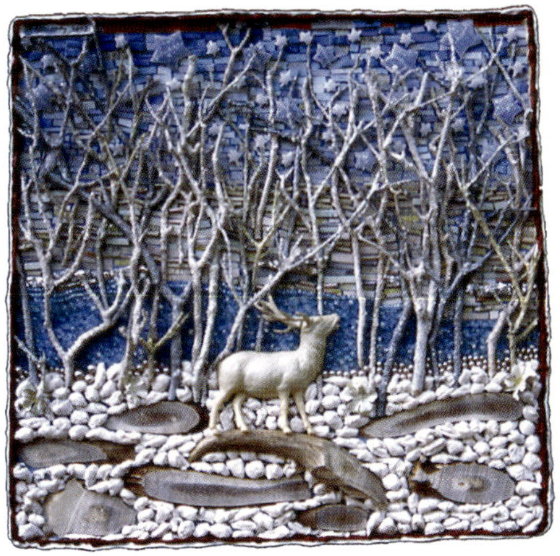

MOON COLD, MOON HOT 2003, 12 1/4 x 12 1/4 MIXED MEDIA COLLAGE ON PAPER

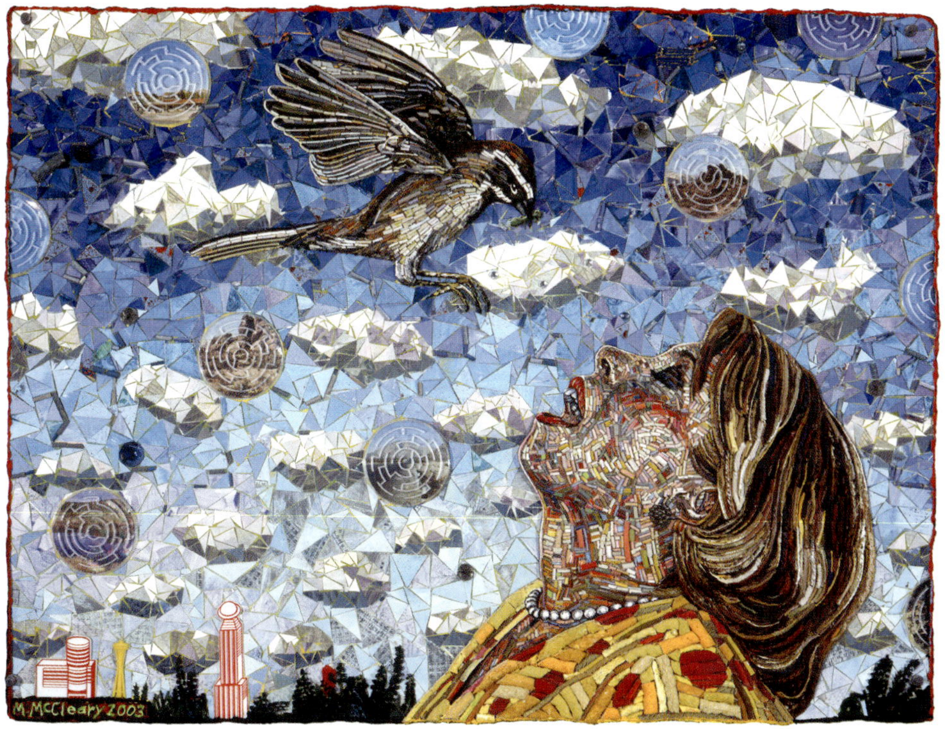

LULLABY 2003, 22 3/4 x 30 1/4 MIXED MEDIA COLLAGE ON PAPER

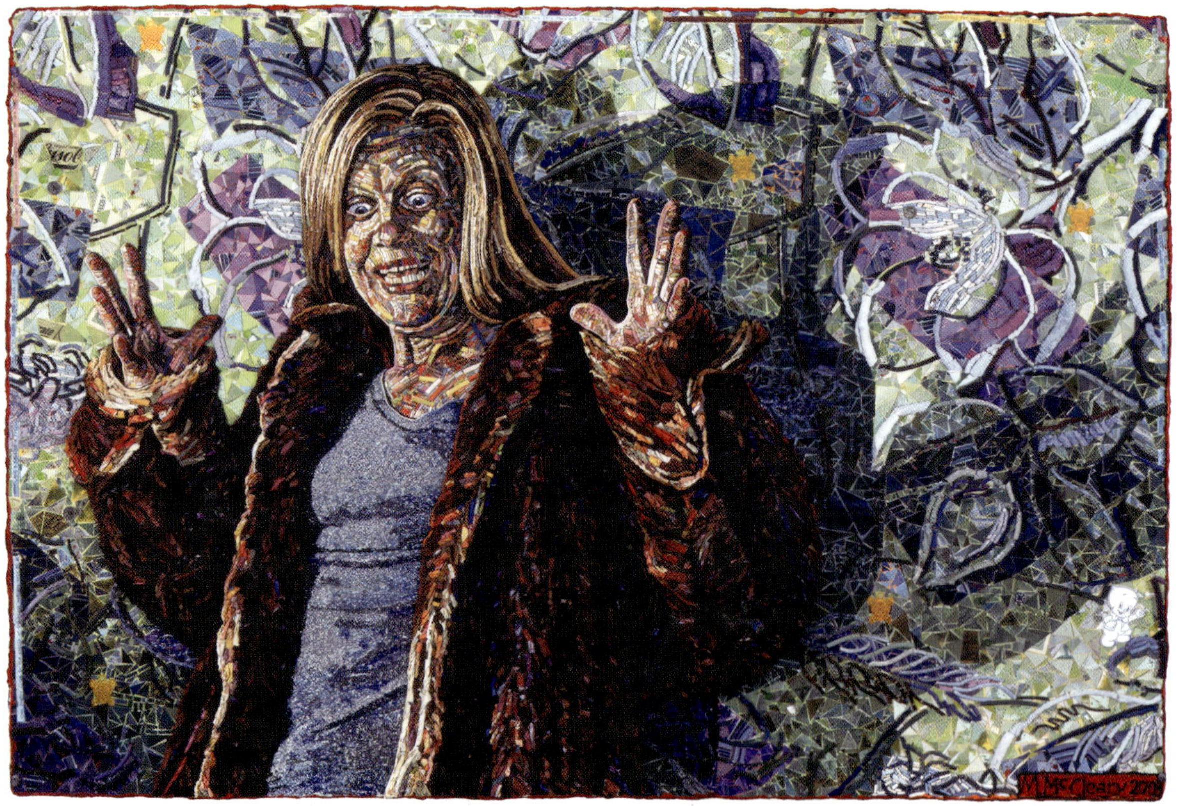

THE HOO-HAAS 2003, 30 1/2 x 45 1/2
MIXED MEDIA COLLAGE ON PAPER

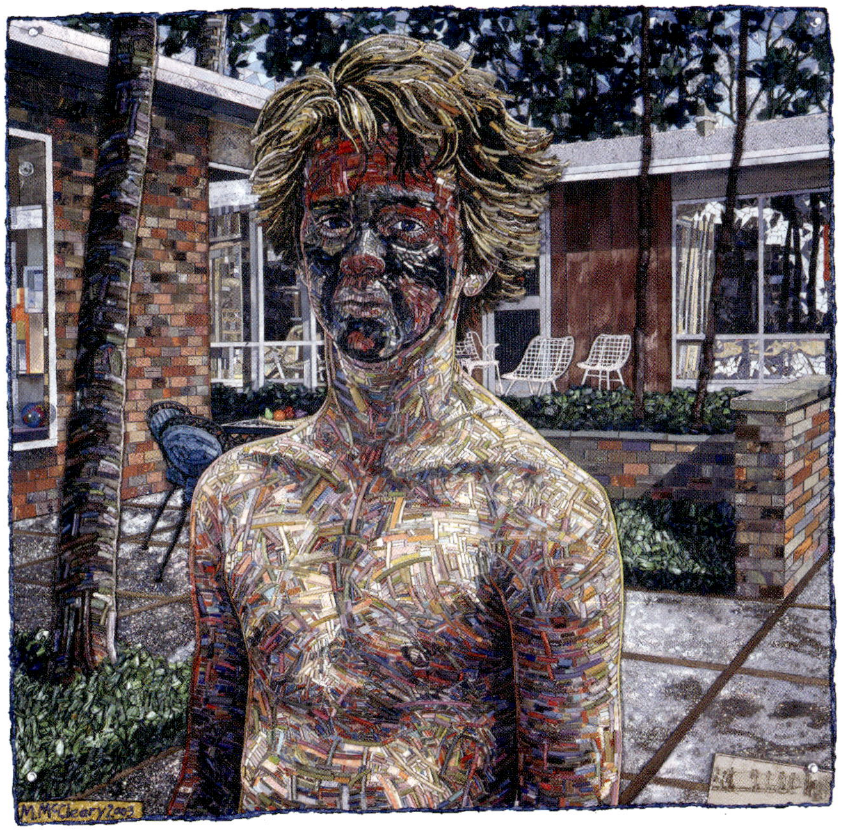

JERUSALEM, ATHENS, ALEXANDRIA, VIENNA, LONDON 2003,
31 1/4 x 31 1/4 MIXED MEDIA COLLAGE ON PAPER

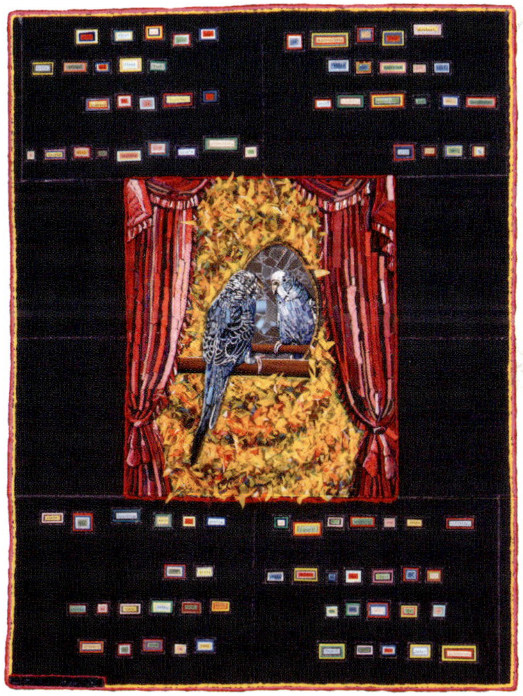

PARAKEET 2004, 30 x 20
MIXED MEDIA COLLAGE ON PAPER

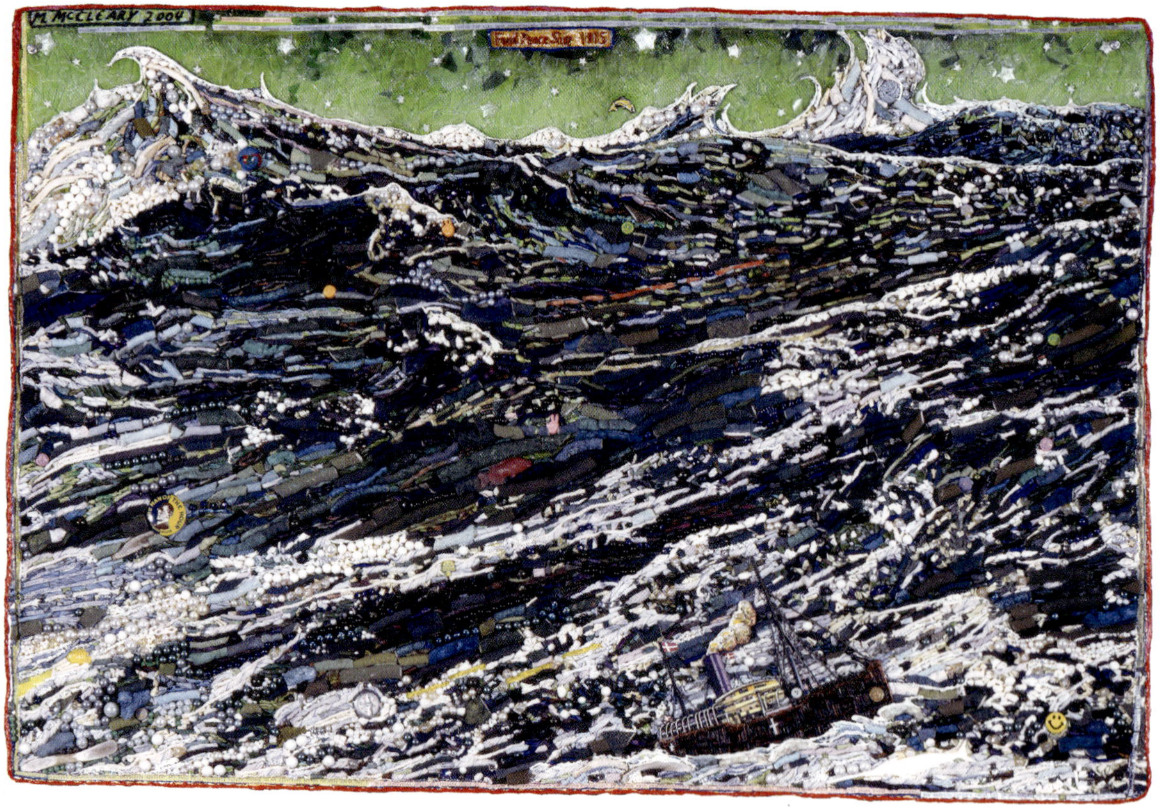

HENRY FORDS PEACE SHIP 2004, 30 x 44
MIXED MEDIA COLLAGE ON PAPER

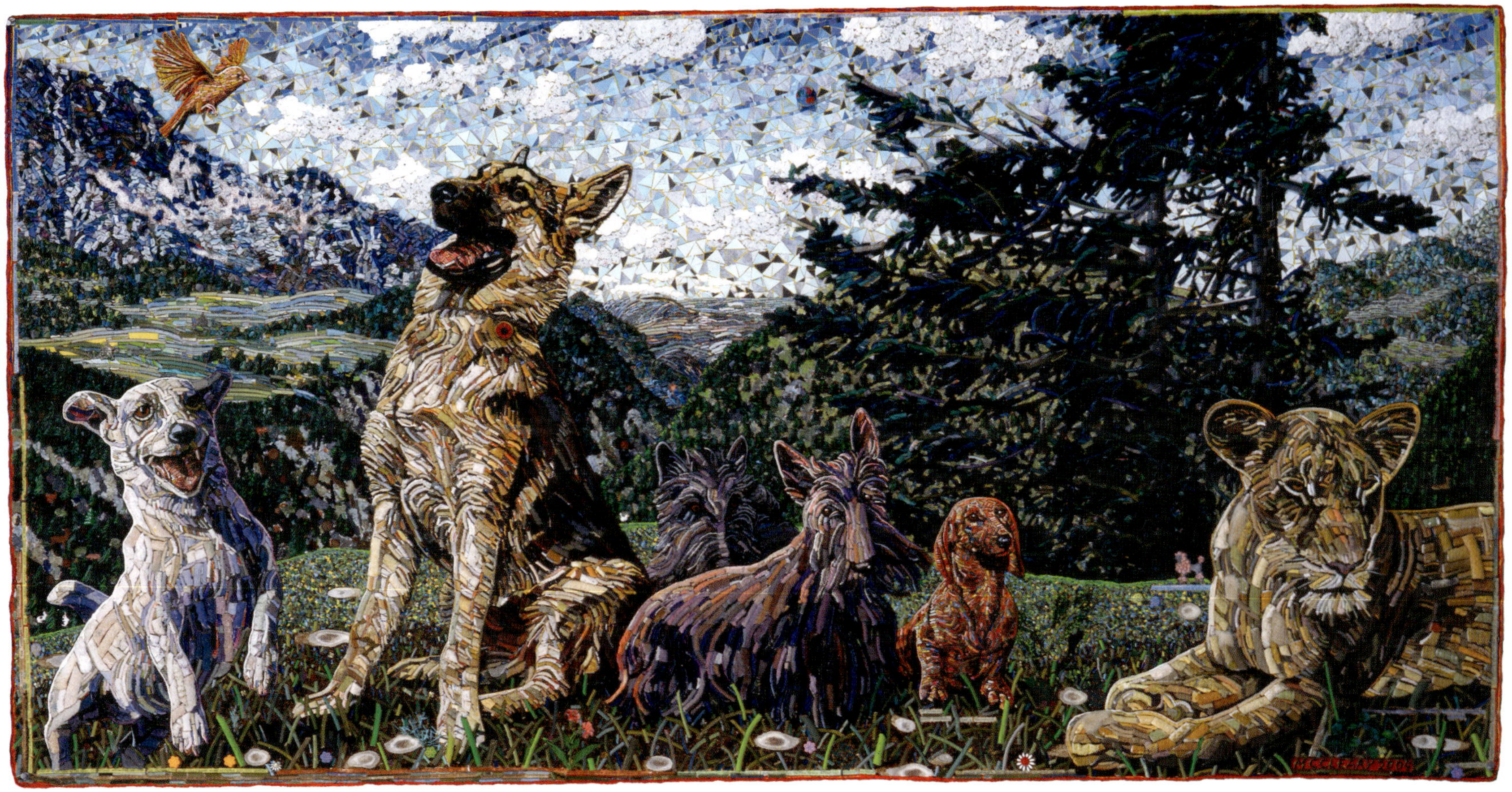

NAZI PETS 2004, 36 x 71 1/2
MIXED MEDIA COLLAGE ON PAPER

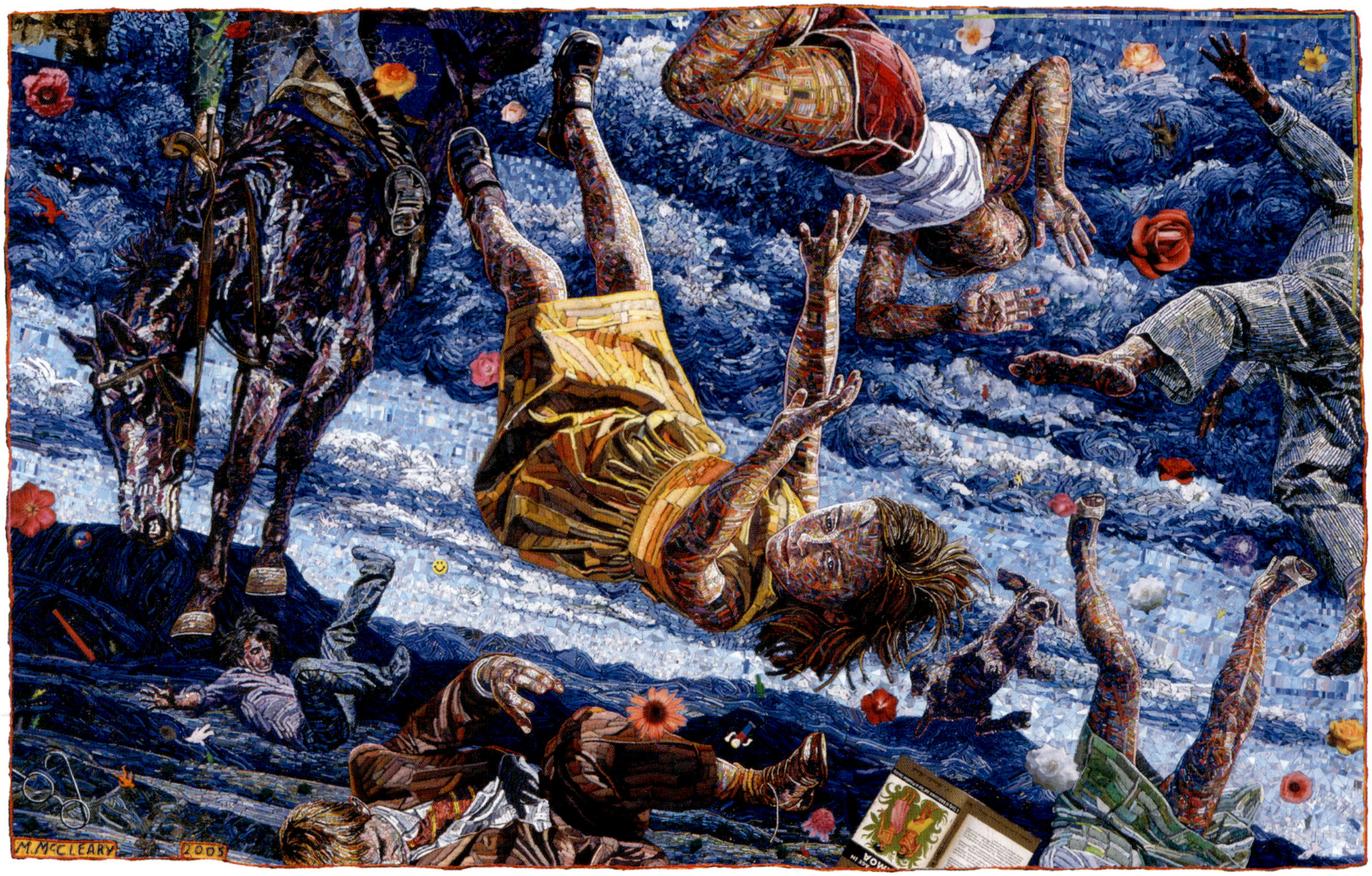

9.81 METERS PER SECOND PER SECOND 2005, 45 x 71 1/2
MIXED MEDIA COLLAGE ON PAPER

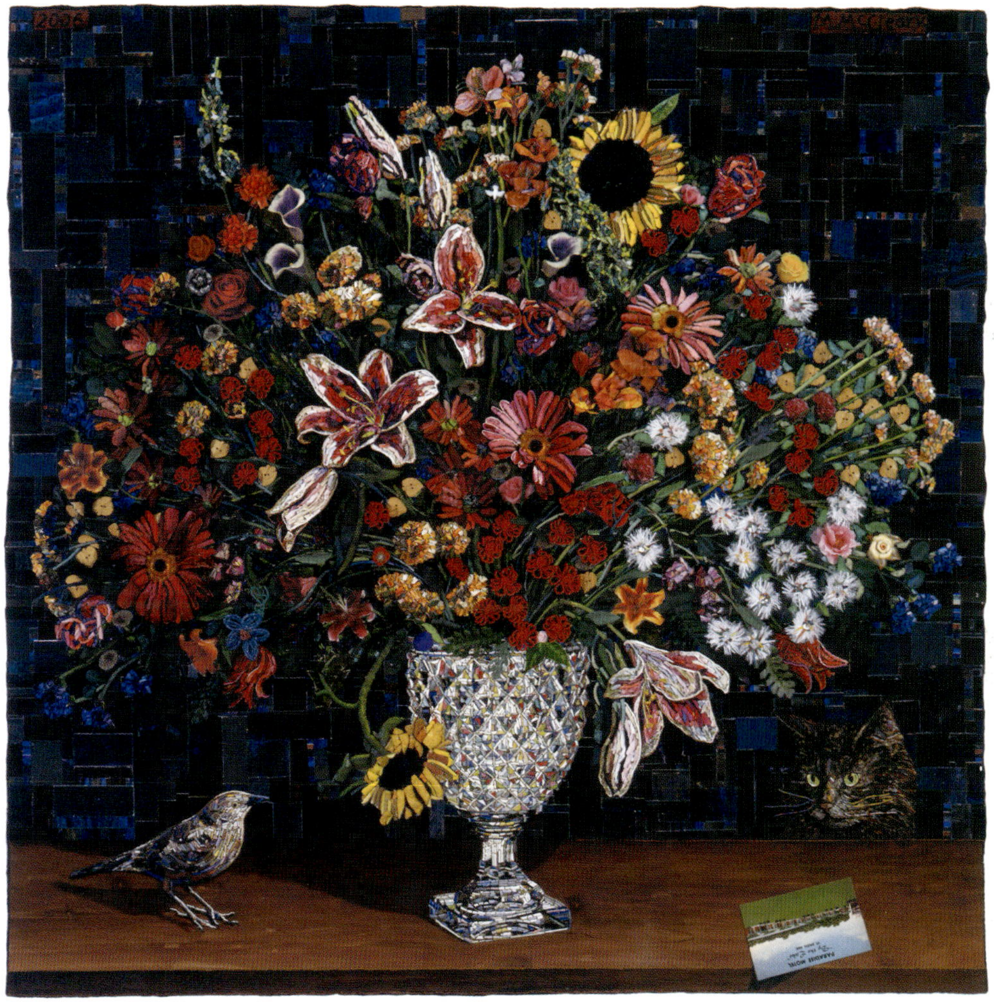

SEHNSUCHT 2006, 45 x 45
MIXED MEDIA COLLAGE ON PAPER

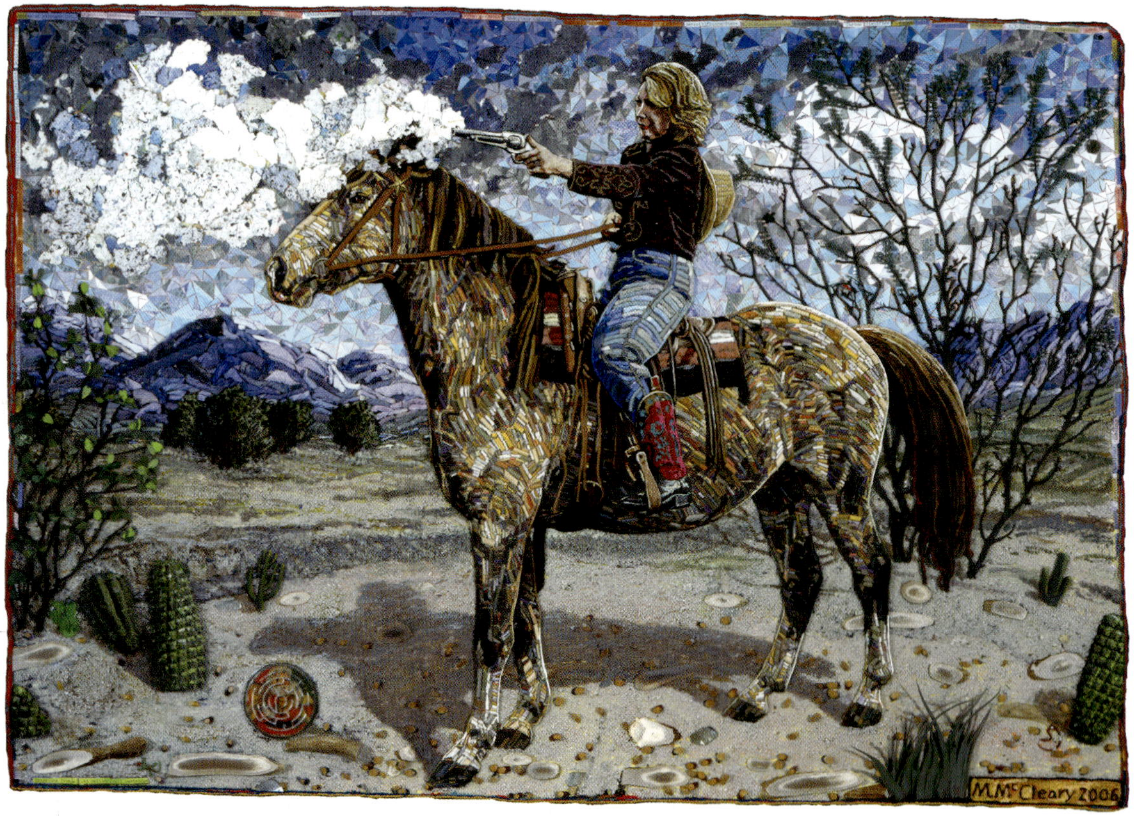

THE STRANGE DUST FROM OUR ACTIONS DRIFTS AND SETTLES UPON US 2006, 30 1/4 x 43 1/2
MIXED MEDIA COLLAGE ON PAPER

Following is a listing of the pieces featured in this catalog, and, when applicable, the text found in the works is in **bold** along with editorial statements in *italics*.

P4 FALLEN, FALLEN, LIGHT RENEW

2005, 15 1/2 x 19 1/2 *Moody Gallery*

P4 BETWEEN DARKNESS AND LIGHT

2005, 15 1/2 x 19 1/2 *Moody Gallery*

P9 PORTRAIT OF JOHN MARMADUKE

1998, 27 x 30 *Collection John H. Marmaduke*

Text at lower middle reads:
Be True to the Dreams of Your Youth

P9 PORTRAIT OF CLINT WILLOUR

2000, 23 x 24 3/8 *Collection Clint Willour*

P10 WHEN SPARROWS FELL

2001, 45 x 67 3/4 *Private Collection*

Information for the text around the perimeter of the collage is from Jasper Becker's Hungry Ghosts: Mao's Secret Famine. *New York: The Free Press, 1996:*
In 1958, Mao Zedong and the CCP decided China's harvest would be greater if sparrows did not eat as much of it every year, so the people were commanded to kill all the birds. Mobilized like a gigantic army, thousands upon thousands of peasants advanced in lines across the countryside banging pots and pans, driving before them sparrows and other birds, until the creatures dropped with exhaustion only to be beaten to death. Movies document smiling peasants watching as truckload after truckload of dead birds were hauled away. The following year, without the birds to prey on them, insects multiplied and ate all the crops. The resulting famine was one of the worst in history, taking an estimated 30 million lives.

Text in the upper portion of the work is from the song, "Lullaby of Birdland," (Words: George David Weiss, Music: George Shearing):
Lullaby of birdland that's what I always hear when you sigh.
Never in my wordland could there be ways to reveal, in a phrase, how I feel!
Have you ever heard two turtledoves bill and coo when they love?
That's the kind of magic music we make with our lips when we kiss!
And there's a weepy old willow, he really knows how to cry.
That's how I'd cry on my pillow if you should tell me farewell and goodbye!

Text on the bottom right side is from the old hymn "His Eye is On the Sparrow." (Words: Civilla D. Martin, Music: Charles Gabriel):
His eye is on the sparrow, and I know he watches me.

Verses from Matthew10:29–31 are at the bottom:
Are not two sparrows sold for one cent? And yet not one of them will fall to the ground apart from your Father. But the very hairs of your head are numbered. Therefore do not fear, you are of more value than many sparrows.

The background of When Sparrows Fell *is a reversed image of the Ming Dynasty painting,* Ch'iu Ying Landscape in the Manner of Li T'Ang (Sung Dynasty), *ink and color on paper, Freer Gallery of Art, Washington, D.C.*

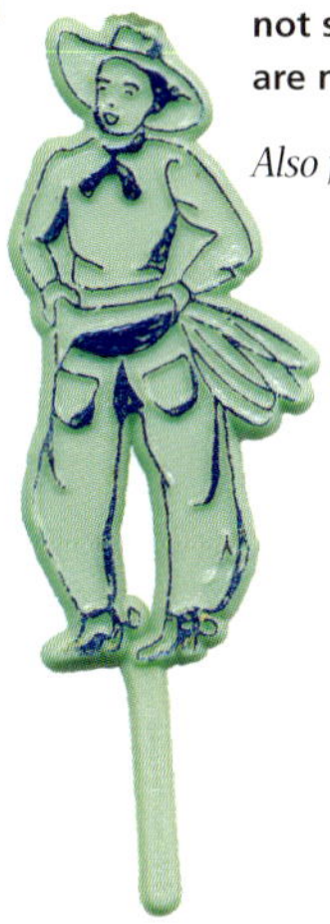

P11 ALLEGORY OF THE SENSES

2002, 48 x 72 7/8 *Collection of the artist*

Text in the upper right quadrant is from the song, "Dancing in the Dark" (Words: Howard Dietz, Music: Arthur Schwartz):
Dancing in the dark, till the tune ends
we're dancing in the dark, and it soon ends.
We're waltzing in the wonder of why we're here.
Time hurries by; we're here and gone,
looking for the light of a new love
to brighten up the night. I have you, love,
and we can face the music together, dancing in the dark.

Text around the perimeter is from 2 Corinthians 4:18:
While we look not at the things which are seen, but the things which are not seen: for the things which are seen are temporal, but the things which are not seen are eternal.

Also from I John 1:1:
That which was from the beginning, which we have heard, which we have seen with our eyes, which we have looked at and our hands have touched—this we proclaim concerning the Word of life.

P12 THE FIRE AND THE ROSE

2003, 7 3/8 x 5 1/2 *Private Collection*

From T.S. Eliot's Little Gidding:

And all shall be well and
All manner of thing shall be well
When the tongues of flame are in-folded
Into the crowned knot of fire
And the fire and the rose are one.

P12 BEYOND THE BONE

2003, 4 1/4 x 6 *Private Collection*

Text is from T.S. Eliot's Landscapes, IV. Rannoch, by Glencoe:

Memory is strong beyond the bone.

P12 MOURNING DOVE

2003, 16 x 16 *Collection Camille and Locke Bryan*

P13 MOON COLD, MOON HOT

2003, 12 1/4 x 12 1/4 *Private Collection*

Text is from T.S. Eliot's Landscapes, IV. Rannoch, by Glencoe:

Substance crumbles, in the thin air/ Moon cold or moon hot.

P13 LULLABY

2003, 22 3/4 x 30 1/4 *Collection Alison L. Smith and Dean A. Burkhardt*

P14 THE HOO-HAAS

2003, 30 1/2 x 45 1/2 *Moody Gallery*

Text from T.S. Eliot's Sweeney Agonistes: Fragment of an Agon:

When you're alone in the middle of the night and you wake
in a sweat and a hell of a fright
When you're alone in the middle of the bed and you wake
like someone hit you on the head
You've a cream of a nightmare and you've got the
hoo-ha's coming to you.
Hoo hoo hoo
You dreamt you waked up at seven o'clock and it's foggy and
it's damp and it's dawn and it's dark
And you wait for a knock and the turning of a lock for you
know the hangman's waiting for you.
And perhaps you're alive
And perhaps you're dead
Hoo ha ha
Hoo ha ha
Hoo
Hoo
Hoo
KNOCK KNOCK KNOCK
KNOCK KNOCK KNOCK
KNOCK
KNOCK
KNOCK

P15 JERUSALEM, ATHENS, ALEXANDRIA, VIENNA, LONDON

2003, 31 1/4 x 31 1/4 *Collection El Paso Museum of Art*

The text on the collage is from T.S. Eliot's The Waste Land:

Falling towers/Jerusalem, Athens, Alexandria, Vienna, London/Unreal.

Also included is T.S. Eliot's quotation from Joseph Conrad's Heart of Darkness *in the epigraph of* The Hollow Men:

Mistah Kurtz—he dead.

P15 PARAKEET

2004, 30 x 20 *Collection Mary Daniel*

Text reads:

Just about any bird toy is appropriate for your parakeet. Bells, swings and items that allow for exercise are best. However it is important to avoid mirrors, especially for male parakeets. A mirror will so capture your bird's attention, he will not want to leave it, spending each day gazing at himself and avoiding any other activity. Some birds will relate to the image in the mirror as their mate, bond with it and even try to protect it from a real female bird you later introduce.

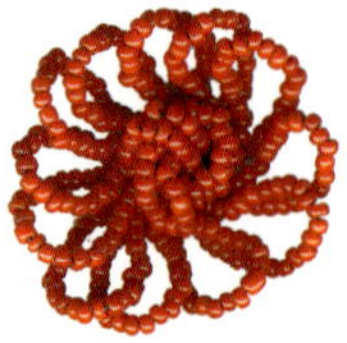

P16 HENRY FORDS PEACE SHIP

2004, 30 x 44 *Collection of June Mattingly and Buck Liptak, Dallas TX*

Information as well as various quotes by Henry Ford within the collage are from taken from Barbara S. Kraft's The Peace Ship. *New York: Macmillan Publishing Co., Inc., 1978:*

On December 4, 1915, Henry Ford and a group of over 150 pacifists, suffragists, educators, settlement workers, ministers, journalists, college students, 4 children, 2 entertainers and one stowaway, as well as others described as "genteel mendicants, inveterate notoriety seekers, main-chance reformers, cheap mountebanks, crackpot philanthropists and boisterous egoists" set sail from Hoboken, N.J. in an ill-fated attempt to stop World War I. This unofficial group of citizens hoped to convene a "conference for continuous mediation" in Europe with representatives from both belligerent and neutral countries who would meet until peace could be arranged. The warring nations could not be persuaded to attend. Ford footed the bill at a cost of $400,000. He commented, "I didn't get much peace, but I heard in Norway that Russia might well become a huge market for tractors soon.

Mme. Rosika Schwimmer and Wanamaker's Department Store were in charge of decorating the ship prior to the trip. In less than a week the lounge and cabin furnishings were redone in chintzes with matching drapes and lampshades and 140m pillows were flung about the premises. The ship's library was replaced with books on peace. A dove with an olive branch in his beak hovered over the portrait of King Oscar II at the entrance of the main salon, which had also been redecorated. The public rooms were transformed with festoons, ferns, palms and flowers, all in red and green to betoken the spirit of Christmas. Stuffed doves, olive branches, flags and Easter lilies surrounded the light fixtures. The ladies' parlor was done in the suffrage colors of yellow and white. Each cabin had a basket of fruit and a potted plant.

In the 1930's a Scottish shipyard sold the ship to the Japanese as scrap iron.

One good way to hinder progress is to fill a man's head with all the learning of the past . . . merely gathering knowledge may become the most useless work a man can do.

Take away the capitalists and you will sweep war from the earth.

I'll bet this ship against a penny that we'll have the boys out of the trenches by Christmas.

I'll buy the Oscar II as a souvenir if we succeed. Somewhere there is a mastermind sending brainwave messages to us.

The only reason why man does not know everything that the human mind has ever learned is that no one has ever yet found it worthwhile to know that much. It is only through misapprehension that men will fight one another.

Verse from Matthew 5:9 at the top edge:

Blessed are the peacemakers.

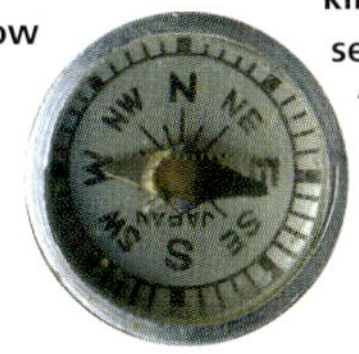

P17 NAZI PETS

2004, 36 x 71 1/2 *Collection Carol Windham*

Text around the perimeter reads:

Nazi leaders were noted for love of their pets. Hitler, a vegetarian and hater of hunting, adored dogs and spent some of his final hours in the company of his Alsatian, Blondi, whom he would take for walks outside the bunker at some danger to himself.

Hitler showed little emotion at the death of friends, but wept when his canary died.

Hitler was given films by a maharaja that displayed animals killing people. The Fuehrer watched with equanimity. During another film showing humans killing animals, Hitler covered his eyes and begged to be told when the slaughter was over.

In the trenches in WW1, the one creature Hitler seemed to care about was a little white terrier, Fuchsl (Foxy), who strayed into the trenches. He taught him how to do tricks and showed delight in the affection the animal showered on him. He refused to sell him, even when offered 200,000 marks.

"Stasi" and "Negri" were two Scottish Terriers given to Eva Braun after her suicide attempt. SS Colonel, Adolf Eichmann had a dachshund. Martin Bormann had a poodle. Nazi's passed a law prohibiting Jews from owning pets.

In April 1933, soon after they had come to power, the Nazis passed laws regulating the slaughter of animals. Later that year Herman Goering announced an end to the "unbearable torture and suffering in animal experiments and threatened to 'commit to concentration camps those who still think they can continue to treat animals as inanimate property." Laws protecting wildlife were also passed. The Nazis were much concerned with endangered species, and Goering set up nature reserves to protect elk, bison, bears and wild horses. He called forests "God's cathedrals." The aim of the Law for the Protection of Animals was "to awaken and strengthen compassion as one of the highest moral values of the German people."

Goering, as head of the Luftwaffe, rained death on Europe, but kept a sign in his Berlin office that read: "He who tortures animals wounds the feelings of the German people." His lion, Caesar, roamed his home, Carinhall, at will.

Bureaucrats at the Nazi Ministry of the Interior conducted research on the kindest methods of killing crustaceans. In 1936 Hitler issued a special decree setting forth regulations for their preparation in all German restaurants.

"Crabs, lobsters and other crustaceans are to be killed by throwing them in rapidly boiling water. When feasible, this should be done individually."

P18 9.81 METERS PER SECOND PER SECOND
2005, 45 x 71 1/2 *Moody Gallery*

Text on upper and right edge reads:
Near the surface of the earth gravity is a downward acceleration. Over time, it causes all unsupported objects to pick up a downward speed. Since gravity is a persistent acceleration, falling objects keep falling faster and faster. For objects near the surface of the earth, gravity causes them to accelerate downward at a constant 9.81 meters (m/sec)/sec. This means each second it falls, it will be traveling 9.81 meters per second faster.

P19 SEHNSUCHT
2006, 45 x 45 *Moody Gallery*

Only text is the title.

P20 THE STRANGE DUST FROM OUR ACTIONS DRIFTS AND SETTLES UPON US
2006, 30 1/4 x 43 1/2 *Moody Gallery*

Text around the perimeter of the collage reads:
Emissions from a .45 caliber ball cartridge: Acenaphthene, Acetonitrile, Acrylonitrile, Aluminum, Antimony, Arsenic, Barium, Benzene, Benzo[a]anthracene, Benzo[b]fluoranthene, Benzo[k]fluoranthene, Benzo[g,h,i]perylene, Benzo[e]pyrene, 1,3-Butadiene, CO2, CO, Carbon disulfide, Chloromethane, Chrysene, Copper, Dibenz[a,h]anthracene, 1,2-Dichloroethane, Dioxin/furan compounds, Ethylbenzene, Ethylene, Fluoranthene, Fluorene, Formaldehyde, 1,2,3,4,7,8-Hexachlorodibenzofuran, Hexane, Hydrogen cyanide, Indeno[1,2,3-cd]pyrene, Lead (Pb), Methane, Methylene chloride, Methyl ethyl ketone, 1,2,3,4,6,7,8,9-Octachlorodibenzofuran, Oxides of nitrogen, Phenanthrene, Propylene, Pyrene, Styrene, Toluene, 1,2,4-Trimethylbenzene, TSP, m-Xylene, p-Xylene, o-Xylene, Zinc

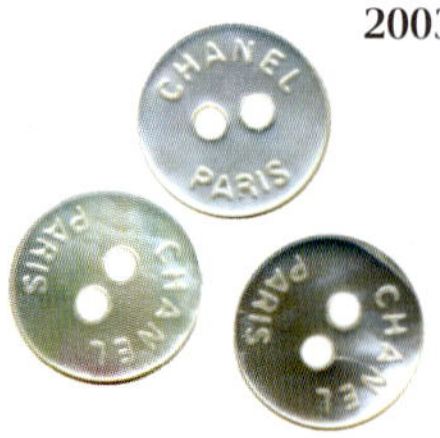

Mary McCleary was born in Houston, Texas in 1951 and studied at Texas Christian University (B.F.A., cum laude, 1972) and the University of Oklahoma, Norman (M.F.A., 1975). McCleary currently lives and works in Nacogdoches, TX. She is retired Regent's Professor of Art at Stephen F. Austin State University.

SELECTED SOLO EXHIBITIONS

2006 *After Paradise, Moody Gallery, Houston, TX*
2003 *Raid on the Inarticulate*, Adair Margo Gallery, El Paso, TX
2001 *Mary McCleary Beginning with the Word, Constructed Narratives: 1985–2000*, Galveston Arts Center, Galveston, TX; Stephen F. Austin State University Art Center, Nacogdoches, TX; Dallas Visual Art Center, Dallas, TX; Art Museum of Southeast Texas, Beaumont, TX; Southwest School of Art & Craft, San Antonio, TX*
2000 *Children of the Apple Tree*, Adair Margo Gallery, El Paso, TX
1998 *Scriptural References*, Amarillo Museum of Art, Amarillo, TX
1995 *Mary McCleary: Parables*, Lynn Goode Gallery, Houston, TX
Mary McCleary: Collages, Brazos Gallery, Richland College, Dallas, TX
1993 *The Living Word*, Adair Margo Gallery, El Paso, TX
1992 *Things Seen, Things Not Seen*, Lynn Goode Gallery, Houston, TX
1989 *Personal Visions*, The Watson Gallery, Houston, TX
1986 *Recent Work: Mary McCleary*, The Watson Gallery, Houston, TX
1985 *Mary McCleary: Mixed Media Constructions and Ceramics*, Mattingly-Baker Gallery, Dallas, TX
Mary McCleary Constructions, Watson/de Nagy Co. Gallery, Houston, TX
1983 *New Works on Paper*, Watson/de Nagy & Co., Houston, TX
1982 *Mixed Media Constructions*, Mattingly-Baker Gallery, Dallas, TX
1980 *Mary McCleary*, Watson/de Nagy & Co., Houston, TX
1978 *Mary McCleary: Introductions*, Watson/de Nagy & Co., Houston, TX
1975 *Mary McCleary Graphics*, The University of Oklahoma Art Museum, Norman, OK

SELECTED GROUP EXHIBITIONS

2006 *I Love the 'Burbs*, Katonah Museum of Art, Katonah, NY*
2005 *Broken Beauty: Figuration, Narrative and the Transcendent in North American Art*, Laguna Museum of Art, Laguna Beach, CA *
Never Done: Women's Work From the Permanent Collection, El Paso Museum of Art, TX
The Next Generation: Contemporary Expressions of Faith, Museum of Biblical Art, New York, NY *
2003 *Bread Upon the Waters* (through 2006), VAM Gallery, Austin, TX; Gallery W, Sacramento, CA; Billy Graham Museum, Wheaton University, Chicago, IL; Whitworth College, Spokane, WA; Evangel College, Springfield, MO; Roberts Wesleyan College, Rochester, NY; Fourth Presbyterian Church, Chicago, IL; Birgen Sandzen Memorial Gallery, Lindborg, KS; Taylor University, Upland IN;

John Brown University, Siloam Springs, AR; Baylor University, Waco, TX; Huntington College, Huntington, IN; Union University, Jackson, TN; Gordon College, Wenham, MA; Asbury College, Wilmore, KY; Visions Gallery, Albany, NY; Yale Institute of Sacred Music, New Haven, CT; Rivier College, Nashua, NH; Hope Church, Austin, TX.

2002 *"Let There Be Light" and Other Works*, Adair Margo Gallery, El Paso, TX
Sugar and Spice, University of Maine at Presque Isle, Presque Isle, Maine

2001 *Re/New*, James Gallery, Houston, TX

2000 *Word as Art: Contemporary Renderings*, Gallery at American Bible Society, New York, NY *
Neo-Rococo, University of Texas at San Antonio Art Gallery, TX

1999 *Texas IV*, Tyler Museum of Art, TX

1998 *The Figure: An Invitational Exhibit*, Valley House Gallery, Dallas, TX
Up Close and Personal, Edith Baker Gallery, Dallas, TX

1997 *The Last Picture Show*, Lynn Goode Gallery, Houston, TX
Establishment & Revelation, Dallas Visual Art Center, TX *
Altered Egos, Hallswalls Gallery, Buffalo, NY *
CIVA Creates the Portrait, Dordt College, Sioux Center, Iowa; Bethel College, St. Paul, MN; Roberts Wesleyan College, Rochester, NY; Gordon College, Wenham, MA; Concordia University, Mequon WI; Calvin College, Grand Rapids, MI; Houghton College, Houghton, NY; and Abilene Christian University, Abilene, TX

1996 *Through a Glass Darkly: Christian Belief in Contemporary Art*, Adair Margo Gallery, El Paso, TX

1995 *Magic and Mystery*, Laguna Gloria Art Museum, Austin, TX
Texas Art for Russia, exhibit organized under the auspices of the American Embassy in Moscow/American Center, the American Consulate, Yekaterinburg and the Art League of Houston; traveled to Yekaterinburg, Tomsk; Russian Museum, St. Petersburg; Rostovondon; Nizhniy-Novgorod; Moscow; and the American Center at the U.S. Embassy *

1994 *Veiled Images*, Art Museum of South Texas, Corpus Christi, TX *
Miniatures: Smallest, Smaller, Small, Hooks-Epstein Galleries, Houston, TX
Portrayals, Galveston Arts Center, TX

1993 *Outside/In: Outsider & Contemporary Artists in Texas*, Laguna Gloria Art Museum, Austin, TX *
Personal Attachments: The Art of Collage/Assemblage, Hooks-Epstein Galleries, Houston, TX
In The Beginning, Art Museum of South East Texas, Beaumont, TX *
Fur, Fins, Feathers & More, Galveston Arts Center, TX

1992 *Second Annual Cross Show*, Lynn Goode Gallery, Houston, TX

1991 *Baubles, Bangles and Mardi Gras Beads*, Galveston Art Center, TX
Cuentos de Mi Vida/Stories of My Life, Adair Margo Gallery, El Paso, TX
House, Laguna Gloria Art Museum, Austin, TX
Silent Stories, Peregrine Gallery, Dallas, TX
Is There Still Life in the Still Life or is Nature Morte?, Galveston Arts Center, TX

1990 *Family Icons*, Peregrine Gallery, Dallas, TX

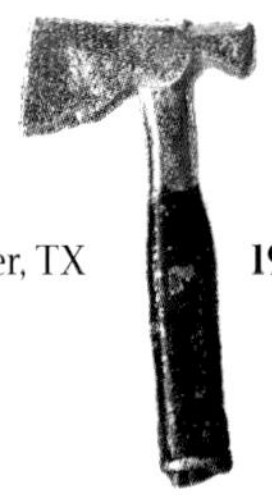

1989 *Mid-America Biennial Art Exhibition*, Nelson-Atkins Museum of Art, Kansas City, MO *
Texas Realism: Legacy II, Art Museum of Southeast Texas, Beaumont, TX *
Review: Ten Years of Women and Their Work, *Women & Their Work*, Austin; traveled to Richland College, Dallas, TX; Texas A&M University Gallery, College Station, TX *

1988 *Works By Women*, Gihon Foundation Collection, Peregrine Gallery, Dallas, TX; Rosenberg Library, Galveston, TX; RGK Foundation, Austin, TX; Midwest Museum of American Art, Elkhart, IN; Mitchell Museum, Mt Vernon, IL
Review / Preview, Watson Gallery, Houston, TX
Invitational, Bernice Steinbaum Gallery, New York, NY
Texas Women, National Museum of Women in the Arts, Washington, DC; traveled to Laguna Gloria Art Museum, Austin, TX *

1987 *Works By Women*, Gihon Foundation Collection, The Museum, Texas Tech University, Lubbock, TX; The Museum of Arts & Sciences, Macon, GA; The Gertrude Herbert Memorial Institute of Art, Augusta, GA
From the Object: Still Life Themes and Variations, Glassell School of Art, Museum of Fine Arts, Houston, TX *
Narrative Painting, Addison-Ripley Gallery, Washington, DC
True Wit: Humor in Texas Art, Cullen Center Gallery, Houston, TX *

1986 *Texas Time Machine*, Cullen Center Gallery, Houston, TX; also The Sheraton Gallery, Dallas, TX. *
Transpositions/Collaborations, San Antonio Art Institute, TX
Platters, Willingheart Gallery, Austin, TX
Piero Fenci, including collaborative work with Mary McCleary, The Front Room Gallery, Nantucket, MA
Works By Women, Gihon Foundation Collection, Plano Cultural Arts Center, TX; University of Dallas, Irving, TX; Wichita State University, Wichita, KS

1985 *Dimensional Paper*, San Antonio Art Institute, TX
Ceramic Invitational, The Farmhouse Gallery, Long Island, NY
Texas Visions: A Celebration of Texas Artists, Art League of Houston at Transco Towers, Houston, TX *
Works By Women, Gihon Foundation Collection, Louisiana State University, Baton Rouge, LA; National Organization of Women, New Orleans, LA; McAllen International Museum, TX; Louisiana Tech University, Ruston, LA; Alexandria Museum, LA; Michelson-Reves Museum of Art, Marshall, TX, Plano Cultural Arts Center, TX; Northern Michigan University, Marquette, MI

1984 *Works By Women*, Gihon Foundation Collection, The Central Exchange, Kansas City, MO; Texas Women's University, Denton; Dallas Public Library, TX; Arkansas Arts Center, Little Rock; Brooks Memorial Art Gallery, Memphis, TN; Center for the Arts, Corpus Christi, TX
Paperworks, Watson/de Nagy & Co., Houston, TX
Clayworks, Watson/de Nagy & Co., Houston, TX

1983 *Sculpture: Five Texas Artists Working in Clay*, Mattingly-Baker Gallery, Dallas, TX
Works By Women, Gihon Foundation Collection, Weil Gallery, Corpus Christi

State University, TX; The Warehouse Living Arts Center, Corsicana, TX; Angelo State University, San Angelo, TX; Museum of the Southwest, Midland, TX; Museum of the Big Ben, Sul Ross State University, Alpine, TX; Firehouse Arts Center, Norman, OK

1982 *Works By Women*, Gihon Foundation Collection, Western Texas College, Snyder; Stephen F. Austin State University, Nacogdoches, TX; Cameron University, Lawton, OK; Victoria Regional Museum, TX; Amarillo Art Center, TX; Texas A&I University, Kingsville; Goddard Art Center, Ardmore, OK; Meadows Art Museum, Shreveport, LA
38th Annual Painting Competition, Abilene Fine Arts Museum, Abilene, TX
Recent Works from East Texas, Tyler Museum & Art Center, TX *

1981 *Three-Dimensional Paintings*, Watson/de Nagy & Co., Houston, TX
Works By Women, Gihon Foundation Collection, Wichita Falls Museum & Art Center, TX; Texas Christian University, Fort Worth, TX; Northwood Institute Art Center, Dallas, TX; Tarleton State University, Stephenville, TX; Abilene Fine Arts Museum, TX

1980 *Made in Texas*, New Orleans Contemporary Arts Center, New Orleans, LA
Works By Women, Gihon Foundation Collection, Southern Methodist University, Dallas, TX; Texas A&M University, College Station, TX; Cultural Arts Center, Temple, TX; Waco Art Center, TX; Tyler Museum & Art Center, TX
Three Person Show, Mattingly-Baker Gallery, Dallas, TX

1979 *Women in Sight: Women and Their Work*, Dougherty Cultural Center, Austin, TX; traveled to Lawndale Annex, University of Houston, TX
Inaugural Group Show, Watson/Willour Gallery, Houston, TX
Made in Texas, Huntington Art Gallery, University of Texas, Austin, TX. *
Paperworks: An Exhibition of Texas Artists, Witte Memorial Museum, San Antonio, TX; also Arlington Community Center, Arlington, TX; Laguna Gloria Art Museum, Austin, TX; Museo de Monterrey, Mexico; Wichita Falls Museum & Art Center, TX *

1978 *Works on Paper: Southwest 1978*, Dallas Museum of Fine Arts, Dallas, TX
Drawings and Prints 1978, Miami University, Oxford, OH
56th Annual National Art Exhibition, Meadows Museum of Art, Shreveport, LA; also in 1977 *
Stockton National 1978—Contemporary Trends in Printmaking and Drawing, University of the Pacific, Stockton, CA
21st Annual Delta Art Exhibition, Arkansas Art Center, Little Rock, AK
15th Joslyn Biennial, Joslyn Art Museum, Omaha, NE
Water Color U.S.A., Springfield Art Museum, MO

1977 *The Amarillo Competition*, Amarillo Art Center, TX
19th Annual National Exhibit of Prints and Drawings, Oklahoma Art Center, Oklahoma City, OK
Southwest Tarrant County Annual, Fort Worth Art Museum, TX; also in 1970, 1975, 1976
20th Annual Delta Art Exhibition, Arkansas Arts Center, Little Rock, AK
Houston Area Exhibition, Blaffer Gallery, University of Houston, TX; also 1975*

1976 *National Print and Drawing Competition*, Davidson College, NC *
17th Dixie Annual, Montgomery Museum of Fine Arts, AL *
46th Annual Exhibition, Springfield Art Museum, MO

1975 *Women In Houston*, Contemporary Arts Museum, Houston, TX
Boston Printmakers 27th Annual National Exhibit, Museum of Fine Arts, Boston, MA *
17th National Exhibition of Drawings and Prints, Oklahoma Art Center, Oklahoma City, OK; also in 1974
35th Oklahoma Artists Annual, Philbrook Art Center, Tulsa, OK; also in 1973 *

1974 *Potsdam Prints — 1974*, New York State University, Potsdam, NY *
16th Annual 8-State Exhibition of Paintings and Sculpture, Oklahoma Art Center, Oklahoma City, OK *
7th Annual Prints, Drawings and Crafts Exhibition, The Arkansas Arts Center, Little Rock, AK *
Los Angeles Printmaking Society 2nd National Print Exhibit, Otis Art Institute Gallery, Los Angeles, CA *
44th Annual Exhibition, Springfield Art Museum, MO *

1973 *Color Print U.S.A.*, Texas Tech University, Lubbock, TX *

1972 *Two-person*, Texas Christian University, Fort Worth, TX

** Denotes catalog*

SELECTED PUBLICATIONS

Bustard, Ned. *It Was Good: Making Art to the Glory of God.* (Second Edition) Baltimore: Square Halo Books, 2006.

Johnson, Ken. "New Artists Who Are Motivated By Faith." *The New York Times*, 19 August 2005, E33.

Prescott, Theodore, et al. *A Broken Beauty.* Grand Rapids: William B. Eerdmans Publishing Company, 2005.

Spatz, Jake. "Gotta Have Faith—Exhibit Catalog More Than a Coffee-table Book." *The DC Examiner*, 14 August 2005.

Pongracz, Patricia, and Wayne Roosa. *The Next Generation: Contemporary Expressions of Faith.* Grand Rapids: William B. Eerdmans Publishing Company, 2005.

Bowden, Sandra, et al. *Faith and Vision: Twenty-Five Years of Christians in the Visual Arts.* Baltimore: Square Halo Books, 2005.

Heller, Ena, et al. *Reluctant Partners: Art and Religion in Dialogue.* New York: The Gallery of the American Bible Society, 2004.

Romaine, James. *Objects of Grace: Essays and Interviews on Creativity and Faith.* Baltimore: Square Halo Books, 2002.

Willour, Clint. "An Obsession With Compulsion." *Artlies*, no. 35 (summer 2002).

Cullum, Jerry. "New Age or the Same Old Model?" *Artlies*, no. 34 (spring 2002).

Mitchell, Charles Dee. "Mary McCleary at Dallas Visual Arts Center." *Art in America* (January 2002).

Goddard, Dan R. "Visual Arts—10 Best." *San Antonio Express-News*, 30 December 2001.

"Mary McCleary." *New American Paintings*, Vol. 36, Wellesley, Massachusetts: The Open Studios Press (fall 2001).

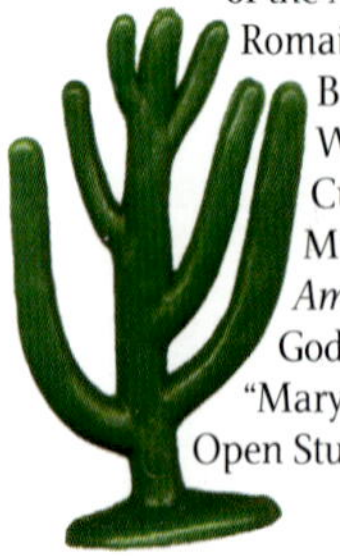

Goddard, Dan R. "Artwork Retell Bible Stories: College Professor's Updated Biblical Images Are Now On Display." *San Antonio Express-News*, 9 October 2001.
Wicker, Christine. "Eyes That See the Glory." *Dallas Morning News*, 26 May 2001.
Mitchell, Charles Dee. "Bible Studies." *Dallas Morning News*, 23 May 2001.
Daniel, Mike, "Mary McCleary at DVAC." *Dallas Morning News*, 13 April 2001.
French, Christopher. "Mary McCleary: Beginning with the Word/ Constructed Narratives." *Artlies*, no. 30 (spring 2001).
Johnson, Patricia. "Best Shows." *Houston Chronicle*, 31 December 2000.
Johnson, Patricia. "Collage Grad." *Houston Chronicle*, 9 December 2000.
Willour, Clint, et al. *Mary McCleary: Beginning With the Word*. Galveston: Galveston Arts Center (2000).
Heller, Ena, et al. *The Word as Art: Contemporary Renderings*. New York: Gallery at the American Bible Society, 2000.
Bonansinga, Kate. "Mary McCleary at Adair Margo Gallery." *Artlies: Texas Art Journal*, no.26, (spring 2000).
"Mary McCleary." *New American Paintings*, No. 24, Wellesley, Massachusetts: The Open Studios Press (November 1999).
Roosa, Wayne. "A Fullness of Vision: The Collages of Mary McCleary." *Image: A Journal of the Arts & Religion*, no. 23 (summer 1999).
Daniel, Mike. "Personal Touch." *Dallas Morning News*, 11 December 1998.
Daniel, Mike. "Go Figure." *Dallas Morning News*, 28 August 1998.
Akhtar, Suzanne. "It Figures." *Ft. Worth Star Telegram*, 28 August 1998.
Ingalls, Hunter. "Exhibition Offers Intriguing Technical Aspects, Naturalness." *Amarillo Globe-News*, 7 June 1998.
"Mary McCleary." *New American Paintings*, No. 12, Wellesley, Massachusetts: The Open Studios Press (October 1997).
Johnson, Patricia C. "Galleries Offer Portraits With Other Themes." *The Houston Chronicle*, 22 December 1995.
Monfrini, Richard Joseph. "Recovering That Which Has Been Lost: A Brief Introduction to the Redemptive Art of Mary Fielding McCleary." *Corum Deo*, vol. 3, no.2 (summer 1995).
Brown, Glen. "Veiled Images." *ArtPapers* (September/October, 1994).
Sherer, Gaye. "Christian Artist Sows the 'Word' Through Her Paintings." *El Paso Herald Post*, 2 December 1993.
Chadwick, Susan. "Biblical Collages Lack Artist's Usual Intensity." *Houston Post*, 18 June 1992.
Johnson, Patricia. "Bible, Greek God inspire Problematic Exhibits." *Houston Chronicle*, 12 June 1992.
Carraro, Francine. "'ReView Translates 10 Years of Progress for Women Artists." *Austin American—Statesman*, 10 November 1989.
Dowell, Susan Stiles. "Big Names and Bright Lights." *Southern Accents*, vol.12, no. 3 (May-June 1989).
Kutner, Janet. "Sketches of 12 Women." *Dallas Morning News*, 15 April 1989.
Smith, Mark. "Laguna Gloria Exhibit Embodies Substance of Women's Souls." *Austin American Statesman*, 23 March 1989.
Bacigalupi, Don. "Houston." *Contemporanea International Art Magazine* (March/April 1989).
Kilian, Michael. "Texas Women's Art Intrigues Washington." *Dallas Morning News*, 31 December 1988.
Kiely, Kathy. "Women Paint Over Texas Clichés." *Houston Post*, 12 December 1988.
Moore, Sylvia, ed. *No Bluebonnets. No Yellow Roses: Essays on Texas Women in the Arts*, Midmarch Arts Press, New York, 1988.
Johnson, Patricia. "Artists in 'Plate Show' Used Unfamiliar Materials." *Houston Chronicle*, 18 December 1987.
Johnson, Patricia. "The Still Life: Is It a Suitable Subject for Painters Today?" *Houston Chronicle*, 18 January 1987.
Chadwick, Susan. "From the Object: Still Life Themes & Variations." *Houston Post*, 18 January 1987.
Johnson, Patricia. "Art: A Sampling of What's Available From Area Galleries." *Houston Chronicle*, 14 December 1986.
Chadwick, Susan. "From the Object: Still Life Themes & Variations." *Houston Post*, 18 January 1987.
Kalmykor, Fran. "Mary McCleary." *Inquirer: Houston's Chronicle of the Arts* (November/December 1986).
Chadwick, Susan. "Garden Variety." *Houston Post*, 24 October 1986.
McCombie, Mel. "Texas Time Machine." *ARTnews* (May 1986).
Chadwick, Susan. "Texas Time Machine." *Houston Post*, 23 March 1986.
McCombie, Mel. "Into The Texas Time Machine." *Artscene* (spring 1986).
Freudenheim, Susan, "Mary McCleary." *Texas Homes* (February 1986).
Johnson, Patricia. "Sesquicentennial Theme Leads To Clichés." *Houston Chronicle*, 25 January 1986.
Everingham, Carol J. "McCleary Exhibit A Walk Through Eden." *Houston Post*, 22 June 1985.
Lawter, Estella. *Women as Mythmakers: Poetry and Visual Art by 20th Century Women*. Bloomington: Indiana University Press, 1984.
Kutner, Janet. "Sculpture: Five Texas Artists Working in Clay." *Dallas Morning News*, 22 September 1983.
Johnson, Patricia. "3-Dimensional Exhibit Varied." *Houston Chronicle*, 18 September 1981.
Crossley, Mimi. "In the Galleries." *Houston Post*, 18 September 1981.
Jarvis, Ron. "Mary Fielding McCleary at Watson/de Nagy." *Art Voices South* (September/October 1979).
Parks, Glenna. "Paperworks." *San Antonio Express News*, 3 August 1979.
Tennant, Donna, "Exhibition Notes." *Artspace* (summer 1979).
Kalil, Susie. "Houston Galleries Showcase New Talent." *Artweek, 28* July 1979.
Crossley, Mimi. "Art: Introductions '79." *Houston Post*, 15 July 1979.
Moser, Charlotte. "Multi-Gallery Openings Bring Swarms." *Houston Chronicle*, 15 July 1979.
Moser, Charlotte. "Art League Show Turns Up Plenty of Texas Talent." *Houston Chronicle*, 9 January 1979.

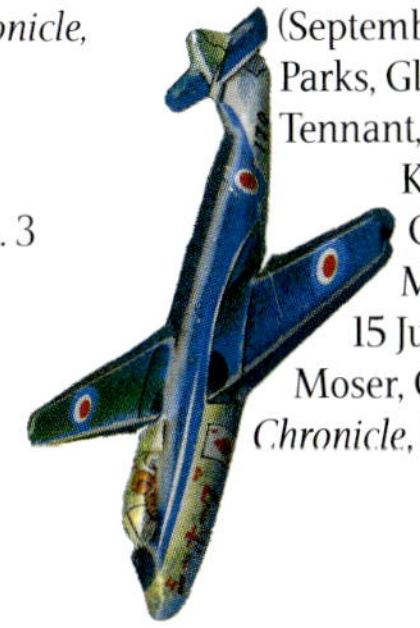

Lee, Edwy B. "1977 Houston Area Exhibition." *Art Voices/South* (January/February 1978).
Crossley, Mimi. "Rocky Theme Needed." *Houston Post*, 16 October 1977.
Crossley, Mimi. "Art: Area Juried Shows." *Houston Post*, 12 October 1977.
Moser, Charlotte. "Evidence of an Insipient Cultural Conservatism." *Houston Chronicle*, 9 October 1977.
Denton, Jon. "Prints, Drawings Touch Funny Bone." *Daily Oklahoman*, 19 April 1975.

FILMS

From the Heart. Director, Nancy Schreiber. Gihon Foundation, Santa Fe, NM, 1981–82.
The Texas Exhibit at the National Museum of Women in the Arts. Directed by Jackie Wilson. KACV-TV (PBS) Amarillo, TX, 1989

PUBLIC COLLECTIONS

Amaco Production Co., Houston, TX
Art Museum of Southeast Texas, Beaumont, TX
Crain, Caton, James & Womble, Houston, TX
Coopers & Lybrand Co., Houston, TX
El Paso Museum of Art, El Paso, TX
Fidelity Management & Research Co., Boston, MA
First International Bank, Houston, TX
Galleria Bank, Houston, TX
Gihon Foundation, Santa Fe, NM
Grand Hotel, Houston, TX
Hastings Entertainment Inc., Amarillo, TX
Hospital Corporation of America, Nashville, TN
IBM, Houston, TX
IBM, Dallas, TX
IBM, Corpus Christi TX
Lackshin-Nathan, Houston, TX
Lufkin Industries, TX
Lufkin National Bank, TX
MBank, Houston, TX
Miami University, Oxford, OH
M/PF Research, Inc., Dallas, TX
Methodist Hospital, Houston, TX
Museum of Fine Arts, Houston, TX
The Pace Collection, New York, NY
Price, Waterhouse, Cooper, Houston, TX
The San Antonio Art Institute, TX
San Antonio Museum of Art, TX
Soghigan & Macuga, Washington, DC
Southwestern Bell Headquarters, Dallas, TX
State of Oklahoma
Temple Emmanuel, Houston, TX
Tulsa City-County Library System, OK
University of Oklahoma Art Museum, Norman, OK
Western Illinois University, Macomb, IL
Wilson Industries, Houston, TX
John D. Williams Company, El Paso, TX

AWARDS

Recipient of a 1988-89 Mid-America Arts Alliance/National Endowment for the Arts Fellowship

REPRESENTED BY

Moody Gallery, Houston, TX
Adair Margo Gallery, El Paso, TX
Flatbed Press, Austin, TX

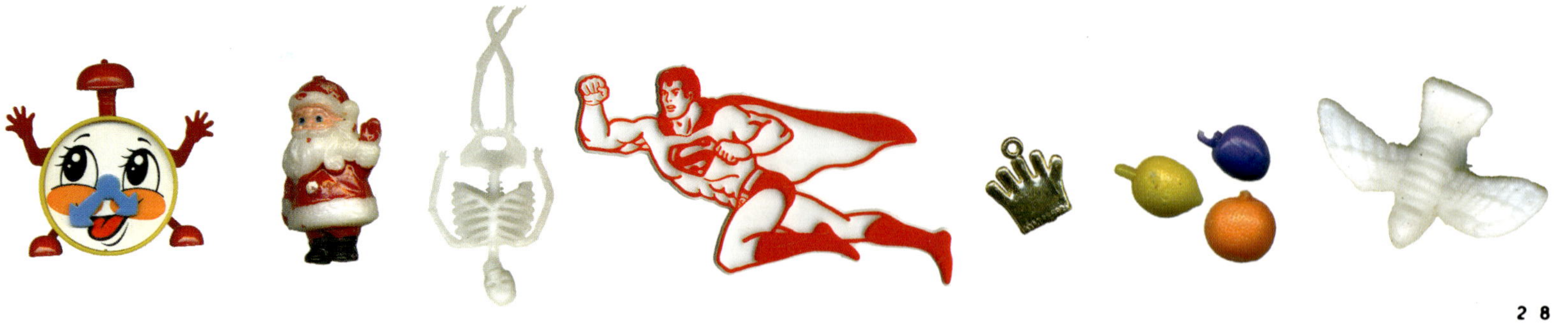